The Arab Woman: Embracing Her Potential

Ruba Rihani

TRANSLATOR: KHOLOUD ZUMOT DIGGS

EDITOR: FRANCES SMYTH-WRIGHT

ISBN-13: 978-9-0595-0268-0

ISBN-13: 978-9-0595-0268-0

DEDICATION

For you, woman; because you are everything.

CONTENTS

FOREWARD

This book consists of seven chapters, each of which begins with a true account of a situation involving a woman living in an Arab country. Although these pictures look dark, there is a glimmer of hope at the end of each chapter that presents a proposal requiring action very soon.

The book begins with the issue of a woman's position within the home as a mother and then discusses her role as the guardian of the family's honor. The book also discusses the status of the woman and her role in the home and society and the prevailing perspective that believes that she is just a painting in the museum of a man. Then the book addresses violence against women in all its forms and how it should be dealt with.

The book also addresses the challenges a woman faces at work in addition to her multiple roles as a wife and working mother. It tackles the psychological effects of the life of oppression that she lives, the factors that lead to it, and her reactions to this deadly disease. Finally, the book presents a proposal to church leaders in the Arab world that sheds light on the Christian woman who continues to suffer under double injustice within the family, society and perhaps the Church, even though God has gifted her with both a distinguished position and a value equal to that of the man.

I sincerely hope that this book will bring about a quantum leap of change in the status of women.

PREFACE

Ruba Rihani Abbassi, an accomplished writer, gives us an in-depth look at the deplorable treatment of Arab women and relates truth as she's experienced it first-hand, with all its raw emotion and pain. At the forefront of the Arab culture is a fiercely dominant patriarch; a patriarch devoid of accountability at the expense of women. Even the smallest details of the anecdotes described in this book leave us shaking in our boots.

In this Arab world, the woman is the protector of the family's honor, but no one wants to admit that it is the man who violates this honor. In extreme circumstances, a young woman is forced to marry the man who robbed her of the most precious thing she had, a longing to gift the person she loves with her virginity.

With a strong instinctive love both for her family and women, Abbassi shows us that a woman is left no choice but to repress her own emotions in order to care for others. Consequently, the culture interprets this surrender as a weakness, but it is this sacrifice that becomes the core of a woman's strength. Why must a woman's worth be understated? Can't the woman be respected since she pushes the cradle with one arm and rocks the world with the other? Abbassi ultimately tells us that the time has come for us to admit that the Woman is the Mother of the Man!

Abbassi writes about all forms of abuse women are subjected to. She then addresses the reasoning behind the violence driven by men toward "the weaker vessel." The power these men use against women is only to satisfy their own selfish needs and thus the self-esteem of women becomes non-existent. The man forgets that the best way to honor his wife is to exalt her.

Abbassi then addresses the working woman's issues. Life circumstances leave her torn between a tyrannical husband and a demanding employer. The unbalanced partnership in marriage surfaces. The Arab man is not ready to contaminate his hands with dish-washing soap and diapers and the working woman must continue this additional duty and she is the one who pays the price. She must "catch-up" to achieve social status at the expense of exhausting her mind, body and soul. It is at that point when the man uses this excuse to satisfy his desires outside of marriage.

Abbassi concludes her book by presenting solutions for change. She uses Christianity as the focal point for this transformation. In a Christian marriage, there is an equal partnership between a man and a woman. In Christianity, a man's love for his wife becomes the true motivation for the wife's submission. A husband cannot expect his wife to submit unless he shows his love for her. That gift will be reciprocated with true loyalty from the wife.

This is a must-read book. The writing is academic but simple. Its lessons encourage us to search within ourselves in honest and transparent ways. Our Arab world is blessed to have a writer with this level of clarity and class in both vision and goal.

Pastor Charles Costa
A Judge in the Evangelical Spiritual Court of Appeals
Beirut, Lebanon

A WORTH UNDERSTATED

Deema's Memories:

I went to sleep that night hugging my tear-soaked pillow and beseeching God in silent cries: "God, why did you make me a girl and not a boy? Do you not see my plight and suffering? How many times must I ask for help when a war is waged against me? Lord, please lift this injustice from me. Please!"

The next day I was awakened by my mother's voice calling me from the living room, "Come on, get up! Make us breakfast and tidy up your brother Kareem's room. Also, don't forget that it is laundry day. You know what that means!" I smiled scornfully and looked around as I heard my mother's voice once again. "All Right!" I said to myself, "I better do what she says quickly before she screams."

My high school exams were about to begin, while my brother Kareem was about to embark on his university exams. The question that was taunting me was how is it that my parents can be so indifferent about my exams and academic future? "Could my brother Kareem be so much more important than me?"

I begged my mother to spare me her nagging requests to be at my brother's beck and call, which she always justified by saying that she couldn't do it because she was too busy cooking and serving my father. Of course she was! Why would things be any different? She, like all the other women, had one sole responsibility: Her Home.

I couldn't focus on my studies because of my mother's constant interruptions. What does she want from me? Why couldn't she leave me alone to study and stop her never-ending demands? It seemed like every time I complained she would rush to give me her familiar cliché answers to lift my spirits. It never occurred to her that the impact of her words was hurtful enough to turn a calm sea into a hurricane within seconds. "You will not fail. You are smart and hardworking. All we need from you is a passing grade." She mocks me with these words. How can it be so easy for her to kill my dreams every single day? "Please mom, don't destroy my dream to become a doctor. Please Lord tell her. Tell her to leave me alone and treat me equally with Kareem, the 'hero' of the household."

When I was done wrestling with thoughts and questions that painfully screamed to the surface of my mind, I went into my room. As I sat on my bed I sprang up immediately thinking that she was going to ask me to help out with more household chores, but instead she looked at me and said: "Stop your constant nagging about finishing your college degree! I told you over and over again that we can only afford to pay for your brother Kareem and you know that at the end of the day you are going to be a stay-at-home wife."

Her words created turmoil within me. My parents are only hoping for a passing grade for me while I am striving for the best in order to study medicine. Yet, they get to determine that my future is only to marry and stay at home. What a way to completely destroy the most precious of my ambitions!

That was a sad day for me. What will become of me? I couldn't hold back my tears and stop my mind from churning. I realized that my hopes were only an illusion, a raging fire of injustice consumed my soul. I feared for my future.

I sat down feeling broken, but my heart was still determined to fully memorize everything in my text books in order to reach my goal.

I was done with my exams and hopeful to get honorable grades, but I was completely oblivious to the news my father was bringing home. My father, that proud Middle Eastern man, walked in ecstatically and showered my mother with the greatest of news:

Finally, his friend Salem has asked for his daughter's hand in marriage to his son Adnan. My mother uttered her approving cries of joy all over the house letting my father know that she shared his happiness. She grilled him about all the details as to his response to Salem and then asked how he planned to break the news to me.

His response was effortless: "I gave him my word that we would announce the engagement as soon as Deema is done with her exams." Their joy that day was like an arrow through my heart that was just the beginning of the suffering that lay ahead of me.

My father's words were filled with pride and boasting that fell like a huge immovable boulder on my soul. Silence fell and then was interrupted by my mother's voice: "I tried to prepare her for the idea of marriage, but she was hoping to finish her education." My father's quick response came so easily to him as he sealed my fate. His words represented the mentality of the majority of people in our eastern society and caused a deep wound in my heart that turned to stone. "What education? The money I saved is only enough for Kareem to finish his education. There will be no discussion on this. She will get married whether she likes it or not!"

My dreams were forever shattered and only my memories would bear witness to them. Injustice was about to befall me.

INTRODUCTION:
If we were to explore women's accomplishments in the Arab world, we will find that in every Arab state there are women who overcame the stormy seas of ignorance and the waves of suppression until they reached the shores of success in business, politics, art, education, law, medicine, security, and other fields. These women have freely utilized their intellect and abilities to bring about change in their society in spite of challenges. They have also succeeded in creating a host of opportunities and resources for other women. We find that even in countries suffering under the burden of war and displacement there are still women who are determined to succeed and overcome the mountains of worn-out tradition, injustice, and abuse facing them.

A famous verse in Arabic can be used to describe the irony of the Arab woman's agony. The verse says:
"Camels who roam the dessert die of thirst while they carry water on their backs."

This is the state of the Arab woman in the twenty-first century. She gives life to all that is around her and in return she barely gets a tiny fraction of what she gives. Life in the Arab world is fraught with all sorts of oppression against women. It is hard to find a single Arab household where a woman is not suffering from something that falls under some sort of dreadful and hateful type of injustice. It would not be an exaggeration to say that there isn't an Arab woman who does not suffer oppression at some point in her lifetime. This one is suffering from favoritism towards her brother for the mere fact that he is a male. Another one has to deal with overprotectiveness so that she is deprived of even setting foot outside the house, while a third was divorced by her husband so that she found herself in the street living on the sidelines of society awaiting another husband to bail her out, and a fourth has to put up with sexual harassment at work or discrimination by her employer.

Anyone who takes the time to study what goes on in Arab society would soon come to realize that what is prevalent in Arab culture is the mindset that places women in a lesser status than men. This is done for no reason other than the mere fact that they are women. Men have the right to do everything, including the right to issue rules and regulations that would guarantee their continued dominance and push women to an increasingly inferior place in society.

This is why the woman today is a victim whose rights are constantly violated. She is a prisoner in her own home; she is sidelined, neglected, and subjected to man's authority, prohibited from speaking on her own behalf, and rulings are issued on her own affairs in her absence. Is this truly the situation of the Arab woman in today's world, or is she really in charge of her own affairs and only gives the appearance of being unjustly treated?

In this book, we will attempt to debunk some widespread clichés and assumptions that define the place of women in society based on the perception of men, the media, or local laws and regulations.

For instance, some Arab countries call for upholding women's rights in theory, but they fail to implement and enforce them in their legal system. There is also the media that actively works to cement and entrench widespread ideas about women in society, but choose to ignore some of the pioneer steps taken by some to achieve equality with men. There are widespread convictions held by many men, both those who issue decisions or who implement them in society, that a woman is a weak and imperfect creature and an unequal partner to a man.

One of the other prevalent misconceptions in Arab society is the conviction that the female is responsible for determining the gender of a child, which completely ignores common modern medical knowledge that the gender of a baby is determined solely by the male sperm, which fertilizes the ova. All of this has left Arab women to live in a state of fear for themselves. They develop a solid conviction that has cost them self-confidence and prompted them to relinquish their basic God-given right to a decent life, education, work, and the chance to pursue a higher calling. It is easy then to conclude that deep-rooted social convictions have rendered mute women's contributions to society as full-fledged citizens.

Let's take a look together at Deema's story:
How many times does her story occur in our Arab society over and over again? In spite of all the progress that our social fabric has undergone and in spite of the growth in standard of living, the idea of associating Arab women with only the home and motherhood has not progressed to meet the demands of this day and age.

Although Deema believed that her right to education was stripped away from her and although she was determined to persist and succeed, marriage was forced upon her and she became a mother of three girls only to be widowed at the age of 28. Her husband suffered a heart attack on the job and no one was able to help him in time. Today Deema and her girls can barely make ends meet living on the meager amount that they receive from social security.

PERCEPTION OF FEMININITY IN ARAB SOCIETY:
A. Vulnerability
The image of the woman in Arab culture is associated with vulnerability and the need for a supporter and protector. This image finds its roots in the nature of the life of ancient Arabs during the time of chivalry and invasion of neighboring tribes. At the time, women were closely linked to one's honor and reputation. It quickly became necessary to hide this creature and defend her against the greed of invaders.

This concept emanates from the idea that in a male-dominated society, a woman became part of a man's assets. She is deprived of the opportunity to develop her skills and abilities and to participate in various aspects of living. Her life becomes confined to the tasks of making a man's life enjoyable and carefree and providing him with male offspring who will follow in his footsteps.

We seem to often recall stories of those women who occasionally excelled in an area that society highly values only because they were fortunate enough to get a better chance than their peers and enjoyed a more generous amount of freedom, which allowed their abilities to shine and to show their true personalities. It became apparent that women, like other human beings, do not lack the courage, eloquence, wisdom, or ability to achieve.

The question here is this: What are the criteria for measuring a women's strength or weakness? Is she truly weak or is she merely deprived of the opportunity to express herself and speak up?

The male and the female are two equal and compatible sides of the same coin in human society. It is true that they differ significantly in their physiology and their social roles. Although the physiological differences cannot be changed, the societal differences came about as a result of a culture created by man through which he enforced his masculine perceptions and worldview on the rest of society.

Traditionally, men would compete with each other and fight in order to gain favor and win a woman's hand in marriage. It was men who fought in battles, wars, and conflicts. Women were warned against falling victim to or participating in these activities. Thus the strength of women lay in using ruses or kindness with men to get their way. To this day, women remain the more conservative gender when it comes to dealing with society and with the human tendency toward violence.

Women endure so much more of life's burdens, challenges, and difficulties. These differences between men and women become much more pronounced once a woman becomes a mother and her maternal instinct takes over. A woman who gives life truly understands it's value and the importance of protecting it and she begins to leverage her strong emotions to protect society from it's evil bent toward barbarism and tyranny. If society were left to its own devices, it would have eliminated the gender of women within a few decades if that were even possible.

The hegemony of the male in Arab society is a strange phenomenon that has dire consequences for both men and women, for it paralyzes our entire society. However, it is so prevalent and familiar that it has become very much part and parcel of the fabric of culture for many men. Not only that, but you see them bragging among their peers. They may even spar with one another verbally on who rules his home with a bigger iron fist and who is the tougher, more controlling man of women's private lives using various means, from the day a woman is born until she becomes a young woman and a wife.

It can even lead to using insulting and humiliating practices against her. The problem is exacerbated when society blesses these practices and finds legal ways to support and justify them. Men in non-Arab societies have - for the most part - gotten over the desire to control and subjugate women. Why do Arab men continue to feel the need to use all the tools at their disposal to control such a supposedly weak creature? Are women truly the weaker gender?

Studies on women's abilities and their physiological and emotional makeup have shown that she is just about the most resilient creature on the face of the earth. She has an incredible ability to thrive, endure, empathize, and accommodate others around her. At the same time, she is the more flexible gender and more capable of understanding conflicting emotions. If this is true, the question that comes to mind is why then, has she come under the curse of all these trials and tribulations over the centuries? Where is her alleged resilience?

In other words, how could the stronger become the weaker? Perhaps the more painful question here is: If the woman is the more resilient and the one who can endure more hardship, how did the man take the rein of control? Where do women stand on this issue? How did we come to a state where the one who is reared and raised by a woman becomes the one to control her? How did history over the centuries get away with portraying women in the image of a weak, fragile, and broken human being?

B. Subordination

This quality is closely linked to the previous one of vulnerability. According to society, if a woman is vulnerable and is in constant need of support and protection, then she will never be able to depend on herself and to run her own affairs. She will not handle herself well and therefore she cannot be independent and will always need someone to be responsible for her.

Society further promotes such notions through common proverbs and sayings such as:

"Having a man to lean on is better than having just a wall."

This means that no matter how insignificant a man is, his mere existence in a woman's life is much better than without.

There are certain notions that dominate our Arab society that make the man directly responsible for the family and that make his shadow or the protection he provides a necessity for the very survival of the woman and it becomes her shield and shelter. And so over history, a woman was annexed to the man and she no longer was allowed to express her opinion on crucial matters.

She became the recipient of actions, and no longer a doer. Her experiences shrank and became confined to the household, for she was prohibited from participating in public life. Perhaps if these same women today were given the freedom to choose their path, they would not change a single thing about their lives. This is simply because they no longer have the tools or the resources to change because they know only what they are allowed to learn. What can they do now after becoming so used to being only a dependent and a subordinate? A woman in our Arab society is no more than so-and-so's daughter, wife, or mother. Nothing else!

C. A Second-Class Citizen

Since the dawn of the patriarchal age, the woman has become a secondary individual and a second-degree human being. The man single-handedly controlled economic, political, and social duties and left home affairs to women, but they were still under his authority and subject to his whims and desires.

Increasingly over the past few years, Arab women have begun to enjoy a little education and manage to get outside employment, but this happened because of necessity and not because of a change in the Arab mindset. The majority of Arabs still, to a large degree, believe that education and employment for women is a luxury and not a necessity. As soon as there is an indicator somewhere on the horizon for a marriage opportunity, a woman is quickly encouraged to ditch education or employment. Is the fact that she received education or obtained employment enough progress if we know that the mentality has not changed, for the woman is still seen as dependent and a second-degree person? Is she treated equally with her male peers at work? Do working women truly gain economic independence, which is the basis for any kind of independence in society?

Women's inferior status is not confined to the social aspect only, but it extends to the political, legal, and economic realms as well. However, in this book we are focused on the social aspect, particularly the role of the woman in the home as we saw it demonstrated in the case of Kareem and Deema's mother. Her life revolved around serving her husband and doing her household chores. I believe that a woman's endeavor to change her status in Arab society is a long and arduous journey and there are no guarantees whatsoever.

Since the onset of the "Arab Spring" and the formation of the Islamic State (ISIS), not to mention laws issued by governments and practiced by individuals, we have seen that any possible change in the status quo has been foiled. The position of women has moved back to Square One in countries ruled by ideologies that are resistant to change and tolerance toward diversity.

Worn-out and tribal traditions have wronged the woman and so men subjugated her and counted her along with their belongings. Men counted their assets as cattle, poultry, furniture, and women. She never took her rightful place in Arab society and she was not given the freedom of choice in any of her own affairs, including marriage; particularly marriages consummated to serve political, economic, and social interests.

The term "second-class citizen" will always describe the status of the Arab woman unless there is a political will and serious determination on the part of governments and regimes to put forward strategies to empower women and set out to alter gender stereotypes. This is the only way that this effort will amount to anything more than empty words.

D. Fear of the Female

In addition to the male-dominated society stripping women's rights away, it also imposed on her an incredible number of restrictions and taboos lest she attempt to redeem what she lost. (Perhaps this powerless being may one day find the strength to rise again!) Hence, the distorted stereotypical treatment of women that society tries to carve out and instill in the collective social consciousness is that of keeping this creature under control and to never empower her to regain any confidence. So many of our sayings and pop culture stories reflect this way of thinking and are then handed down from one generation to the next. They depict an image of a woman who is driven by her desire and lust without any social restriction or self-deterrence or any regard for values and codes of moral conduct. In these depictions, she makes her decisions based on blind emotion without using her intellect. Her weapons are deception and tears, which often lead to sedition, instability, and the like.

It is easy to see these portrayals of women in Arabic literature and popular sayings. At the heart of the stories in One Thousand and One Nights is the inherent treachery of women. A famous Arab verse talks about women being naturally unfaithful and full of betrayal. Even in their religious rhetoric, religious leaders affirm that the majority of people in hell are women. Thanks to technology these days, such statements become religious rulings and are uploaded on personal phones and computers and are seen everywhere through social media, which instill these ideas in the minds of both men and women alike. Herein lies the more serious danger. Such fatwas (religious rulings) reinforce a man's negative perception of women and cause him to be wary of the women in his life.

One popular saying goes, "Women's tricks outdid Satan's tricks."

Another says, "Listen to a woman, but never take her advice,"

And others say, "A conversation between two women is capable of destroying two homes." "If your sister dies, your honor is preserved,"

And "The mother of a boy is doing well while the mother of a girl is in trouble,"

All these sayings affirm that a woman's place is her home and her kitchen and nowhere else.

One proverb says, "Even if a woman goes all the way to Mars, at the end of the day her place is cooking by the stove."

Today we are facing a crisis of distortion of the image of the woman – an honorable creature who should be an equal partner with the man in building upon the earth and making it a place worthy of inhabiting. This distorted image has penetrated male Arab mentality and has sentenced the female to collective capital punishment. Society in its entirety never bothered to rectify the situation and open its mind and the woman continues to be seen as lacking and insufficient in intellect and in performing her religious duty. She continues to be perceived as a person who cannot control her lust and desire and who, therefore, must be restrained lest she dishonor her dignified family's good name.

E. Gender Discrimination
My mother had four girls one after the other and every time she got pregnant, she wished for a boy to carry the family name and preserve her wealth. When she finally had my baby brother, he became the spoiled little brother whose wishes were our commands. My mother's attitude was no different from other Arab women who favored their sons over their daughters.

This is a reality in our society with families living near and far. Girls are treated like a socially-despicable being. The less-than-favorable reactions toward the arrival of a newborn baby girl that we see in men today take us back to those days in tribal history when men, if given the news that their wife just delivered a baby girl, faces turned black and remained angry for quite a while. This is only one aspect of the Arab attitude towards the female gender passed down to us through heritage since the dawn of Arab society.

This discrimination against women extends to impact women through all the stages of her life. It is a prevalent social practice. It is still quite common to marry a girl off at a very early age in places like Yemen, the Egyptian and Syrian countrysides, and some Gulf countries where education rates are lower and economic burdens are heavier. A Yemeni academic study in 2008 showed that 52% of Yemeni girls were married under the age of 15 while only 7% of boys were married at the same age. The percentage of illiteracy goes up among women who are minors and married to 43%.

There was a news report that went viral all over social media and some local media outlets about an eight-year old Yemeni girl named Rawan who died because of deep wounds on her wedding night. She was married off to a man in his forties. His sexual drive led him to marry this child and the doctor's report said that she suffered deep wounds and tears in her uterus and genitals. Her mother said that the little girl had no clue what being married meant sexually.

In places of work, discrimination is practiced in the form of giving women lower wages for the same work that men do in large sectors of the economy. Once married, a women hands over the reins to the man and she begins to play the role of the follower. A woman may be prohibited from working if her husband is well-off financially. Her private life and personal interests take a backseat and her life becomes completely dedicated to making the life of the man (her husband) easier. In all likelihood, after a few years, such a family produces a similar family who will be entrenched with the same values and raise their children upholding the same traditions. In marriages where there is a dispute between the spouses, the laws themselves are never fair to the wife. They most likely guarantee the man the right to remain in control and to humiliate the woman by imposing conditions that force her in most cases to come back to him in full obedience and submission.

We easily notice this discrimination and its impact through the popular sayings and proverbs that have been engraved in people's minds. The anguish is easily seen on the faces of women striving to bear a son to a man who is not satisfied with four or five girls and so the woman must continue to live with the disgrace while the man keeps trying to prove his virility. He may even go so far as to marry other women just to fulfill this passion while knowing full well that it is his sperm alone that determines the gender of the baby.

Gender discrimination continues in places where we notice that the presence of women is rare; such as decision-making institutions and the more influential professional positions in society. What is strange in all of these circumstances is that the man who degrades and humiliates women on a daily basis - whether consciously or not – and defends the existence of unjust laws and traditions, is the same man who was carried, reared, nurtured, and raised by a woman. He may brag about his mother every now and then and in his mind, he considers her different than the rest of the female gender!

ARAB FEMINISM IN MODERN TIMES:
A. Accomplishments or Failures?

It appears to me that the unfair treatment of women is a never-ending saga. The scenes and episodes may differ from one era to the next, but the narrative goes on and does not change. Although the woman has always been the protagonist, unfortunately she never really finds anyone cheering her on. On the contrary, she is met with suppression, injustice, and blows to the face. Over the centuries, man has worked actively to subdue the woman and shrink her role and enslave her and her helpless children. Today, a woman's status is not much different from that of the 20th century and her circumstances in the Arab world are not much different from the way they were in the past. As a matter of fact, I find that in the third millennium a woman's social, economic, political, and educational status has even regressed. How is that possible?

There have been several concerted attempts led by Arab governments to try and the elevate the status of woman and to give her opportunities to enhance her role in the public (society) and the private (family) sectors. For instance, in 2013 the first all-female legal practice operated by four women was inaugurated. This was the first step of its kind in Saudi Arabia that sparked a long controversy revolving around women practicing law in the first place, let alone an all-female legal practice. In spite of everything, they managed to obtain a license to practice from the Ministry of Justice. As a result, the number of Saudi women working in the legal sector has tripled over the past three years.

Although admirable, these advances have not resulted in the alteration of the male mentality very much. Education policies and opportunities, the legal system and employment opportunities are all still extremely limited and the root cause of the problem has not been addressed. This is why things have remained as they are and changes are merely superficial.

There may be some differences in the circumstances of women of the Gulf region compared to those of the Mediterranean basin from an economic standpoint. The former enjoy privilege and economic prosperity much more than the latter. Their social status on the other hand is similar in so many respects, particularly when it comes to laws regarding divorce, marriage, inheritance, and the right to vote. Some Arab countries are ahead of others in allowing their female citizens who are married to a foreigner the right to impart citizenship to her children irrespective of her husband's nationality. These countries are: Tunisia, Algeria, Libya, Yemen, The United Arab Emirates, and Iraq. Jordanian women have finally obtained some prerogatives after many years of struggle for a bare minimum amount of rights.

There is no excuse for depriving a mother the right to impart her citizenship to her children other than the reality of total discrimination against women. What kind of country pushes its female citizens aside and tries to find exceptions to and issue laws that serve only the interests of males? A woman's inability to impart citizenship to her children extends beyond marriage. It applies also in the case of divorce and herein lies the biggest disaster of all, because divorce cancels her motherhood completely and puts the woman in a boundless dilemma without the hope of a solution.

Arab women are sick of this reality, which although admitted and acknowledged – remains in the realm of wishes and desires. Women continue to await true change that eliminates laws that justify their unfair treatment as citizens. We women tend to blame others and to hold them responsible for our own mistakes. We consider others our stumbling block and consider them guilty for failing to understand us and to appreciate the painful circumstances we have undergone. We ought to first have tried to understand ourselves, or at least developed an awareness and a correct assessment of past trials. This is precisely the huge roadblock that Arab women have been facing since the beginning of time to this day. The biggest responsibility of all is ours to bear in leading the struggle to regain our rights and bring about change to the social mindset and to strive for fairness in laws and opportunities.

B. Fake Modernism

Armand Able (a Belgian academic and Islamic Scholar) once said: "Educating women does not mean creating a bigger distance between men and women. It just means dividing up the cake into equal pieces."

We need to understand that we as women do not aspire to be an identical coin to the man. We just want to be the other side of the same coin. Throughout the years as Arab society was opening up to the rest of the world, we failed to recognize that equality and justice between men and women means that each of them would play a different role and in the correct manner that is consistent with their physiological and psychological makeup. This does not mean that we give each of them a role and prevent one of them from performing it. We need to come to the understanding that a difference on the outside does not necessarily reflect a difference on the inside. Women today are fully capable of occupying all positions in all areas and walks of life. Getting to this stage was no easy task. Women have worked hard to accomplish this and many women around the world have paid a price for those times where women's status was facing the opposite direction from that of the man.

The rate of educated women has seen a rise in the Arab world because now the number of educated women is equal to – if not higher than – the number of educated men. On the surface of things, this gives us a positive indication that life is progressing and moving forward and puts our hearts at ease regarding the future of coming generations.

What is perplexing however, is that in spite of all these higher rates and despite all the accomplishments that women have achieved today, we continue to suffer from being looked down upon as in the past. Women continue to be seen as a service-provider or a limited human being. Let me even put it differently: We continue to hold on to age-old perceptions that see the man as the stronger sex. What is so sad is that many Arab girls and women today see themselves in that same demeaning light and with the same sense of inferiority.

REFERENCES

1. A Collection of Russian Writers, "Materialistic Materialism and Historical Materialism" translated by Khairi Al-Damin, Moscow, Progress House 1975, page 277
2. [Pikshtatoviski and others: Unrecognized writer], Ethics Science, Moscow, Progress House 1990, page 31
3. Firas Al-Sawwah, "The Mystery of Ishtar" eighth edition, Dar Alaeddin, Damascus 2002
4. Simone De Beauvoir, "The Second Sex", The Modern Library for Printing and Publishing, Beirut 1979
5. Ulydov, "Social Awareness" translated by Basheer Al-Siba'i, Dar Ibn Khaldun Publishing House, Beirut 1972, page 287
6. Muhsin Jassim Al-Mousawi, "A Thousand Nights and A Night Society".
7. Sahar Khalifah, "Memoirs of Unrealistic Woman", Al-Adab House for Publishing and Distribution, Beirut 1992.
8. Abd Al-Ghani Salamah, "The Effects of the Arab Spring on the Arab Woman", The Modern Dialogue, vol. 3677 3/24/2012 www.alhewar.org
9. https://maktoob.helwa.yahoo.com/063923677-html
10. http://www.ahewar.org/debat/show.art.asp?aid=177599

THE GUARDIAN OF THE FAMILY'S HONOR

Eman: Buried Alive

She sat all clothed in black. Her mourning clothes were supposed to be an indication of grief at the death of her husband, but her face instead showed anguished confusion. Should she frown to look truly sad because custom and tradition deem that she ought to be? Should she be thinking of the funeral arrangements, the burial, and the mourning period she was about to embark upon or should she be thinking of her duty to show hospitality toward those coming to pay their respects? She began to ponder the fact that she was now a widow and the new challenges that were to come with this status? She began to review her entire life and the years of suffering that had managed to kill any sentiment within her. It didn't make a difference anymore! Life was nowhere to be found in her crushed soul.

She recalled her marriage and how for years she lived in a constantly tense atmosphere where she was always told what to do. She had lived with an internal debate about what was permissible or not until she could no longer tell the difference. She had been told that a married woman should do this and should not do that in order to not bring shame upon her husband. She was told that no matter what she thought she ought to obey her husband and never raise her voice or speak if others were present with him because that would be shameful. It was undignified to leave the house because she should only be serving and caring for her husband. Rather than his wife she was his slave. She could not leave the house without a chaperone for fear of what people would say. After she married this old disabled man, she considered finishing her education in order to build her skills because she did not want the shame of being divorced, for that title in itself was fraught with disgrace and dishonor. She agreed to marry the late

Nabil just to avoid shame. How could a divorcee thrive in a society that did not accept her existence and sees her as a disgrace?

After her first miserable marriage where she was held hostage in her home by an abusive, gambling drunkard, she had gotten a divorce. She thought that she was finally free but had fallen into another trap. On the one hand, her family was treating her like a burdensome disgrace and on the other hand, society was watching her, pointing fingers and raising all sorts of questions every time she did anything. Why all this? Because she and her divorce were both a disgrace. Even other women feared socializing with a divorcee to protect their reputations. What would people say if they socialized with or received her into their homes? Why would a married woman bring upon herself a bad reputation and being the subject of gossip? Married women saw her as a threat to their marriages. She had become a living example of all the proverbs that cautioned about "loose and promiscuous women".

The most painful thought was what would become of her life. Was there no one who could save her? Even at the peak of her youth when she was dreaming of her knight in shining armor (a forbidden dream in her society), she found herself succumbing to her family's pressure to accept the first suitor who knocked on her family's door only because that was the proper way to begin a courtship in Arab society. No matter who the man is, everyone agrees with the Arabic saying that "having a man to lean on is better than having nothing but a wall." Nevertheless, she decided to be patient and to make the best of her engagement. But every time she would go anywhere, her brother would be right in the middle between her and her fiancée. She felt suffocated with no power to address the situation. The entire engagement was spent tending to traditional feasts and protocols that never gave her the opportunity to really get to know the proposed "protector and guardian of her honor." Her parents gladly tolerated all the pressure put upon her from outside the home. This pressure came from the traditions that the opinion of the paternal uncle should be respected (even if he never consulted with her family) the formal visitations by the elders of both families, and the opinion of the maternal uncle. These were beautiful traditions but where was her opinion considered at all? Where was her voice?

Everyone dictated how she lived her life and she just concurred; otherwise she would be dishonoring the family. When she was a student, she faced a barrage of questions every day: "Where were you? Why were you late? Who called you? Who is this girl you are spending time with? What would people say about us?" She wondered if they cared at all about the real person inside her. She did not understand what her existence meant to them. She was lost in all these superficial, empty appearances and worn-out traditions. She kept thinking to herself; "How long will society continue to define my life and control me and my family? How long can I withstand this in silence?"

Then when she entered the workforce to prove herself and to learn how to be mature, she had to limit her relationships with male colleagues in order to be seen as a respectable woman. Every word she uttered could be held against her and anything that she did could be perceived as improper or disgraceful.

As a teenager, she had nobody in her family who was interested in listening. How could she express her fears as she watched her body change and grow and was told over and over that talking about such matters was inappropriate? She heard her Mom speak of her intimate relationship with her Dad as a taboo and necessary evil in order to conceive children. If she was curious about anything sexual, she would respond by saying: 'It's inappropriate to bring up subjects of this sort."

The "inappropriate" label applied to every aspect of her life and dominated conversations concerning behavior. So she found difficulty expressing herself because she was never given the opportunity to speak up. The instructions to her brothers were no exception to this refusal to acknowledge emotion, for they were told that it was shameful for men to cry, and they too bottled up the most sincere and honorable of human emotions. Surely, unless this vicious cycle is broken, they were doomed to pass these notions on to their children who in turn will perpetuate curses rather than blessings.

Once the internal monologue was over, the widow finally woke up and returned to her reality only to find that that it had not changed. She was fully a prisoner to a cycle that would be too hard to ever change.

When I think about Eman's story, the end of a lobster's life comes to mind. This beautiful sea creature is thrown alive into boiling water until cooked and offered as a delicacy to seafood lovers. Eman too, was buried alive by worshipped cultural practices that ooze out of the walls of every home.

THE ARAB CULTURE
When we consider the image of women in any Arabic society, we find that several factors influence our perceptions and those are not associated with religious heritage as much as social attitudes and values that are inherited by everyone, irrespective of religious or minority groups. This

stereotype of women that is prevalent in Arab societies has given rise to the painful status quo that smothers women and tightens the noose around their femininity, roles, dreams, and abilities. These attitudes lead us to ask: "Are Arab women happy with their roles, or would they rather be men, given the restraints placed on their lives?"

I am one of those Arab women who grew up hearing my family wish that I were a boy and not a girl. I thought I was the only one on the face of the earth who heard such things from her parents. Then as an adult, I worked with other women and discovered that millions of women all over the Arab world faced rejection merely because they were born female and not male.

This means that similar customs, traditions, and common practices in the Arab world impact the lives of Arab women everywhere. One of these is the overprotection of women. In the eyes of society, women are the weakest link, fragile, easily damaged and incapable of making their way through life on their own. Women have strictly-defined roles: mothers and homemakers. This means that women need men in every stage of their lives, and in return they need to preserve the honor and reputation of these men. Arab society poisons young girls' minds from the day they are born with the idea that their very birth and existence is a disgrace to the family. When Arabs congratulate someone on the birth of a female baby, they say "may God compensate you with a boy next time." And if a man has another baby girl, he automatically gains the title "father of girls" which is used as a derogatory term.

EVERY YOUNG GIRLS' OBSESSION
I was speaking to a relative of mine who had immigrated to the United States ten years ago. At the time, he said to me: "Now that my daughter Noor has grown into this beautiful young woman and has a respectable occupation at a good company, my only true wish is to see her married to a man who would shield and protect her (the Arab word used here is "sutrah", usually associated with the marriage of girls. The word literally means to cover up imperfections or blemishes). I froze in place while listening to him on the phone. I replied: "Tell me something, what wrong has she done that you seek to cover up?" He asked: "What do you mean?" I said: "Did you not say you wanted to marry Noor to one who can cover up her shortcomings? In the same breath, you also said that she is beautiful and enjoys a great position in her company. What disgrace has she committed that needs covering up? He was stunned at my question and hesitated before responding. Then he said: "I meant no harm, and my daughter certainly has done nothing that would disgrace her! Its just an expression we say about girls once they reach the age of marriage."

The word "sutra" has become every young woman's preoccupation. You hear the word uttered by both male and female. You hear it from father, mother, brother, aunts, uncles and everyone who is related to a young woman in any way, shape. or form. So, she grows up thinking that she is some sort of a mistake or imperfection that needs to be hidden. Girls have no idea that this word has distorted their image in society and has reinforced their humiliation and marginalization, in addition to granting a husband rights to discipline her and do with her as he pleases. Why not, since he takes all the credit for being the hero who was man enough to cover up all the blemishes found in her femininity? What more could she want? By the way, both my brother and I were raised together in a Christian home living in a predominantly Arab Islamic society. This does not mean that we are from Mars and have a different view on women. This culture of taboos still leaves its shadow hanging over everyone. Please come and visit our Christian homes and you will find the same set of core cultural values and attitudes engraved deeply on the very fabric of our belief system. It is true that not all girls are forced into marriage without their consent. What saddens me is that when a girl is given the freedom to choose or reject a marriage proposal, she chooses a husband out of her desire to cover her shortcomings because society wants her to be shielded and protected, and not because she has reached a level of intellectual or emotional maturity or because she has made wise life-choices.

If only I could take every girl by the hand and tell her that she is not a blemish, needing to be shielded and covered, having to marry out of necessity, and that she does not have to listen to the hurtful phrases of relatives or friends of the family that hold her hostage to one single viewpoint. I wish I could look into the eyes of every girl and ask her: Do you realize, my dear, how pure, perfect, inspiring, accomplished, and creative you are? Do you understand the importance of your existence in society and the importance of changing all these ideas about you? Who is going to do it if not you? One day you may become a wife and mother and then you will pass on these hurtful ideas to your sons and daughters who will repeat this sad history. What you ought to be doing is creating a new history with a healthy mindset that is free of any accusation or stereotype that does not befit you. If marriage were a shield and a protection, what about divorcees? Why did marriage not shield and protect them? Instead, it threw them on the side of the road filled with anger and bitterness toward men and the institution of marriage.

SEX EDUCATION AND THE CONCEPT OF TABOO

As young Arab men and women leave childhood behind they have passed puberty and reach the marital age without any direction, awareness, education, and necessary information about their bodies, physical changes and the sexual intimacy that awaits them. But we have the internet at our fingertips for both men and women, educated and uneducated. This technology causes so many innocent people to unwittingly fall victim to the forbidden fruit of pornography when they were only curious about sexual matters in the first place.

Many marital relationships are unfulfilling because Arab women are taught that the expression of their sexual needs, which is their human right, is shameful and appropriate only for men. Why is it the man's right and not the right of the woman? Why is it that she has to be coy and reserved in her relationship with her husband? She does not initiate intimacy to risk being misunderstood and is deprived of the enjoyment of sexual relations. She would simply feel guilty if she did.

Arab society has compelled both genders to resort to secretive ways to learn about sex because we have failed to provide the proper education to our young people. Although sex education is a science that is directly connected to human physiological and psychological health, in our Arab countries it is considered a social taboo. The result is that thousands of children are sexually abused because of their ignorance about their own reproductive system and because they lack the knowledge that they need to protect themselves against abusers. If parents took the time to educate their children, many instances of childhood rape could be prevented.

THE NIGHT OF HORROR

The wedding night, or as the Islamic society refers to it as the "night of entry", is one of the most significant nights in the life of every young man and woman. It is something of a dream for so many young people. They dream of it day and night. However, such a topic is almost never discussed in detail in our Middle Eastern societies except with utmost secrecy and through young people whispering about it among themselves.

Because the topic is handled with such ignorance and reservation, young women anticipate the night of their wedding with horror. A reporter from the London-based electronic newspaper Elaf interviewed several Palestinian women. A lady who is identified as Um Muhammad (in a society that revers children, Arab women are normally referred to as Um, meaning mother of their first-born male, as opposed to their first and last name) who has been married for 20 years said that she did not know anything about marital sexual relations and the wedding night was the horror she feared. All she knew was that a lot of blood should flow once penetration took place. She endured heavy bleeding for three days without knowing that this was abnormal. She spoke about the tradition that took place at the time whereby her mother-in-law stood outside the door and waited until her son the groom came out with a white piece of cloth that had blood on it, so she could announce her son's victory to the world with resounding cheers.

As the years went by, this Um Muhammad lady had sons and daughters. She was asked about the extent to which she discussed sexual intimacy with her sons and daughters. She said that she never did because this topic was off limits and not to be discussed. "This is how we were raised," she said.

Asked whether she helped educate her daughter and prepare her mentally and psychologically before she was to be married, Um Muhammad said: "My daughter will go through the experience herself and will find out everything there is to know for herself." When asked about whether or not she had talked to her daughter about the tearing of the hymen and whether she should expect to see blood, the mother said that many years into her marriage she learned that blood may not necessarily appear as a result of intercourse, but it was not possible to change traditional expectations because the mother-in-law will always be outside the bedroom waiting to announce her son's virility and his success in ending the bride's virginity. She wondered: "How can we ever change these assumptions and how can anyone be convinced that it is perfectly normal if no blood at all results from the encounter?"

Statistics show that about 20% of girls do not see any blood at the first sexual encounter and therefore we cannot depend on seeing blood at the tearing of the hymen on the wedding night as the only proof of virginity. When it was explained to Um Muhammad that bleeding may not necessarily happen at the first sexual encounter, that the hymen may only be fully torn when the women gives birth for the first time, and that if there were significant bleeding at the first sexual encounter then that is an indication that the wife has endured sexual violence, she was shocked, and her response was: "Who is going to convince the mother-in-law that this is true?" She went on to say: "Change of attitudes would require awareness programs to be established that cater to young people who are about to embark on marriage as well as mothers-in-law. This would help protect women and put an end to the abuse they undergo under the pretext of proving their virginity."

Yes, this still goes on today in our Arab homes, particularly in the countryside. We cannot measure success in changing these traditions by focusing on a small percentage who's attitudes have caught up with the times after moving to live in big cities. We have a major responsibility to change this painful reality in which women are living. Rectifying these misconceptions is the responsibility of the individual, the family and the rest of society.

THE FAITHFUL GUARDIAN

The concept of honor in our Arab society is associated with maintaining a good reputation and earning the respect and appreciation of others. This is closely tied to controlling the female in our society and ensuring that she remains within the parameters of society's expectations because she is seen as the responsibility of the male as opposed to being responsible for herself and her own actions. It is easy to see here that society goes to an extreme in protecting what it perceives to be important and impactful. The more a society loses control over its own affairs, the more it wants to control the weak, so it can balance its own sense of loss. Therefore, the list of restrictions imposed on women continues to grow. A society that is in crisis and is unable to stand up to confront life-and-death issues such as liberation from unsatisfying occupations, economic problems and high rates of unemployment, will then reduce the concept of honor and dignity to matters that can be fully-controlled. In doing so, society does not realize that in this process it is perpetuating societal dilemmas that ought to be resolved. True honor is actually found in confronting these crises rather than creating and replacing them with insignificant options.

Female virginity is the epitome of honor in our Arab society. In other words, a family's (and by extension a society's) honor, dignity, and reputation depend on a single part of a woman's body. Can you imagine what a huge burden a girl carries on her shoulders from the moment she is born until the day she dies? Why her? Simply because she is a girl. And why is a man not equally responsible for his own honor? Because he is the man, the master, the male who is in control. Nothing shames him and he suffers no consequences.

And how can the man and society condone the man's lack of dignity which already lacks a moral compass? How can he be convinced that if he excelled in protecting his own body from corruption, then his own honor would be preserved and his dignity would be enough?

Would the act of venting his anger really show the importance of that small part of the woman's body as if the only role in his honor is to make sure the woman protects her purity?

Family honor in our society is connected directly to religion. In an Arabic society that has many religions and sects, it is not permissible for a woman to marry a man from a different religion. The occurrence of an inter-religious marriage is a very thorny matter which the government tries to control peacefully to eliminate the consequences that often lead to murder. Anyone who changes their religion and confesses to adopting a new one in our Arabic culture risks being murdered, especially women, more so for honor and reputation than for apostasy. It is very rare that women who change their religion survive death.

I can recall at the age of fourteen receiving the news that a daughter of a family friend named Amal was stabbed to death by her father and brothers because she liked a man from a different religion. This young girl "liked" him only. She did not elope, or marry him. My father came to my room that day steaming with anger and proclaimed: "Did you know that Amal was killed because she didn't protect her family's honor? This will be your fate if you ever think of harming our reputation and marrying one of a different religion!" I felt extreme fear from that straight-forward threat. At the time, I wasn't aware that I was being subjected to psychological abuse. My heart broke for Amal, the friend who paid with her life for the price of admiring a man from another religion.

Divorced women and widows are no exception when it comes to being held accountable for honor. As soon as a woman becomes divorced, she becomes monitored and scrutinized under a political microscope. She is questioned and must be accountable for the sake of honor. If she is seen leaving the house alone, then she would be viewed as searching for a boyfriend or a husband. If she's employed, then she would be accused of not being loyal to her household. If she remained home, then she is a dependent who wastes her time having fun and watching TV. The list goes on and on with many accusations against her.

As for the widow, especially a young one, she wouldn't be any better off than the divorced woman. If a widowed woman stood by the window, then she would be accused of looking for a man. If she visits her friends, then she is not caring about her reputation and honor. If she goes to work, then she is using her sacred body to make money.

These oppressive acts against women have roots in an untouchable patriarchal system whose culture of shame and dishonor continues from one generation to the next. While we expect that the government should take the side of individual freedoms and humanity, instead we find that it is the presenter of accusations. The government, with all its unjust legal systems, stands in alignment with the male, who is the protector of the family's honor. For the man does not care that a soul was robbed of its rights and killed by a hint of a rumor or out of the envy of a jealous heart. It is a death sentence declared by both the family and society.

Here is a story of an Iraqi woman who describes the pain and injustice she experienced under the cover of honor.

The young woman sought refuge with her family in Jordan. She was encouraged to marry a man she wasn't so sure about so that she could maintain dignity and protection. That husband later became the very reason for her humiliation and suffering.

She said: "One day an official from the Labor Department made a surprise visit to my office with a report saying I was working without a permit. I spent that night in a jail cell. I was forced to quit my job. This happened to me over and over again. I began jobs and then was harassed; no returning to Iraq, and no leaving the country. I turned twenty-five years old, hopeless and jobless.

Then our neighbor came, a poor young man with green eyes and red cheeks who followed me every day and sent suitors to ask for my hand in marriage. I kept rejecting him because I knew that as a refugee I wouldn't necessarily make the right choices, but rather pick the easiest one who would give me legal status in my new country. Life is full of ups and downs. I never expected to become a refugee after growing up in a wealthy home and helping those who were in need without expectation. Every day my hardships grew more difficult, more arrests and more harassment came under the name of investigations and overstaying the permit.

My older sisters in Europe had healthy traditional marriages while I stayed with my mother and father. When my middle sister got pregnant, my parents got their visas to visit her and left me alone. All that time, not one good man wanted to marry me except that green-eyed young man. Iraqi expatriate men weren't any better than Jordanian men. They all wanted to have relationships outside of marriage.

Life became unbearable. I became a burden to my parents. I told them I would marry the neighbor (the red-faced one) because he'd been wanting me for years. As a generous Arab man, my father told him he wanted nothing from him, not gold or money, and that all he wanted was a man who would protect his child. So the man rented me a wedding gown and paid for my hair and makeup for the marriage ceremony.

I got married and he became all that I looked forward to. He gave me a new country and fulfilled my dream of stability. I loved him with all my heart, and I still love him. I never kissed or touched anyone else in my life.

I got no congratulations from his family at the wedding. The event, which included the rental of a hall and a dinner for his family and friends, cost my husband a lot of money. I spent the first day of my marriage in a filthy one-bedroom apartment. We didn't even have money to buy breakfast.

In three months, I became pregnant with our first daughter. While I was at the hospital giving birth, my mother-in-law entered my apartment and took all the appliances. I learned later that she took the money as reimbursement for the funds my husband had borrowed for the childbirth expenses. I realized then that I was nothing but a captive.

I went back to working and a new chapter of hardships began. All of my salary towards home expenses went to his mother to pay off the wedding debt, even though she was retired and her house was fully paid. My mother-in-law insulted me every time we met, even in the presence of guests. Nobody ever visited me or invited me to visit them. I lived alone for two years, feeling more desperate and isolated every day. Neither my husband nor my mother-in-law wanted me. They treated me as an inferior being.

My husband was emotionally immature and had a weak character. He lived with a controlling mother. He would leave me for months, not asking about my well-being and never contacted me any time we fought. He was emotionally cold. In short, he was poor in everything; feelings, position, manhood, and intimacy. Numerous times, he hit me and stole my paycheck. Yet, he still maintained his daily prayer duties.

In the midst of my despair, I packed what little I had and traveled to Europe. My sister purchased the tickets for me and my daughter. I brought my son there as well, which allowed me legal residency status. I then had a place to live and a salary. I finished college and obtained my degree in law. Now, I am an intern at a government office. I received my citizenship from this country a year ago.

Ten years have passed since I left Jordan. I will go back to visit, not because I miss it, but to remember that prison in which I lived. This will help me appreciate my freedom even more.

Yes! I finally succeeded, but I have lost the best years of my life which were wasted on people who weren't worthy of being my family.

Honor is not a purity that is to be protected for twenty-five years only to be sold later for any price. Honor is earned through the protection of a woman's humanity and her dignity by a loving family that appreciates her. Honor is a home that provides her citizenship and the opportunity for education and honorable living where she is treated as a human being. Home is sanctuary and love. I have only found that place in a foreign land and from 'kafirs' as my mother-in-law calls them."

And what about the honor of a culture that allows injustice, ignorance, and exploitation, lacking any dignity for its people? What about the state's responsibility in legislating laws that guarantee justice enabling dignity to the citizen regardless of age and sex? Where are we to go from here? Will the injustices against women in our culture always make them vulnerable to inhumane acts? And must injustice be elevated to real violence that attempts to threaten her life, or in many cases, terminate it?

A GLIMPSE OF HOPE

Arab governments document many successes for women in all scientific, social, political, and economic fields. In spite of a culture that limits and humiliates women, they have still been able to climb the ladder and succeed in achieving their goals, reaching the highest positions. Women need to have confidence in themselves and the shame culture is in itself a shame. They will not overcome this patriarchal culture's adversity if we continue to tolerate the status quo.

I would like to discuss my attempt for change through my workshops at the Arab Woman Today Center. I work with small groups of women from different cultural, social, and religious backgrounds. In our monthly meetings, we discuss the faulty social practices that afflict each one of us just for being women. We then move on to discuss ways of reinforcing our role, along with ideas on how to best raise our sons and daughters. We focus on the issues of women's rights, inheritance, sex education, and violence against women. After a long series of discussions, the women build an argument that they can confidently use to overcome their oppressed role, rising above a shame culture that brings them nothing but pain, ignorance, and tyranny.

I am filled with pride when I read about women in all Arab nations taking the initiative to defend their gender. Women in Egypt, Jordan, and

Lebanon are leading the movement for change. I have big hopes for these brilliant young educated women; they yield the fruits of labor for transforming the culture of shame into a culture of respect.

But the process for change will not succeed by just the effort of one woman, or a group of women. The family plays a central role - through its health, economic, social and educational institutions- to the very fabric of society. If the male family member or the male coworker or classmate is not convinced of the need to change the culture as well as the importance of elevating the woman's position, then our efforts will be futile. We merely exist as just a vehicle with no steering capability.

As for institutions, especially the educational ones, changing strategies requires full support, and doing away with backward ideas that continue to marginalize women. Its been too long, and it is time for change. Even if our Arab nations are in political turmoil, the balance of equality and good citizenship must exist.

REFERENCES

1. Adnan Al-Nasser:
   http://www.elaph.com/Web/Health/2012/4/730977.html
2. Ibrahim Othman, "Introduction Into Sociology", Dar Al-Shurooq, pages 2007 pages 89-91.
3. http://www.elaph.com
4. http://www.alghad.com/articles/808736
5. http://uprisingofwomeninthearabworld.org/?lang=en
6. http://uprisingofwomeninthearabworld.org
7. Dr. Muhammad Bin Hassan Addar, "Hymen…Blood May Not Appear with The First Sexual Contact" Riyadh Electronic Newspaper http://www.alriyadh.com/249849
8. Is Bleeding A Condition for Breaking the Hymen? http://www.alamhawae.com/2013/12/blog-post.html

A PIECE OF ART IN A MAN'S EXHIBIT

"I stand here today, staring at a crossroad on a path I know nothing about; a path that appears to be mysterious, scary, and lonely. The choices were never mine. It felt like heaven for a while, then it all turned into hell. I still remember how wonderful our lives were at the beginning, how much he showered me with love, and how charming he was, especially when he needed something. I still remember how he went down on one knee asking me to marry him, touching my heart. I couldn't but say yes.

Day after day, he did everything to please me, regardless of cost. Maybe he impressed me to feed his own ego. When it came to money, he didn't hesitate a bit in lavishing me with expensive clothes. He took me to the most beautiful and expensive restaurants. He turned our house into an exquisite garden. Fascinating me became his art. Of course, his enormous wealth helped. The only condition he put on me was to not visit my family except on holidays. He wanted me to be his and his alone. That feeling numbed me. I can't deny that he truly fascinated me, although I too came from a well-off family with a similar social background as Talal's.

I was that spoiled wife until the jealousy set in that burned deep inside of him. His outbursts were so bad and he wouldn't let me leave the house without him by my side. Even when I needed to go to the market, he would bring the store to our house for me to pick what I wanted. He no longer tolerated me being anything but his property. He controlled everything from my hairstyle to the dress I had to wear. His jealousy was smothering me. I lived in a five-star jail. Everything I needed was available inside my house, because he never wanted me to ever leave the high walls, walls that were carved out just enough for me to see people through the tiny holes.

I can't deny that I loved him to death. I endured it all so that I could stay with him, feeling like a queen wherever I went. I crowned my love and emotions with poems that I wrote him every day. One day to my astonishment, I noticed that he had carved my poems on the walls of our house, making it more of a museum than a house. Honestly, it was that one act of his that caused me to later forgive his shortcomings.

One cloudy day, my life with Talal turned totally upside down. He had received news that his sister had eloped with his lifelong friend who belonged to another religion. The news of her marriage was like a day of mourning for Talal as if she had actually died. He ordered black coffee to be served and announced that there had been a death that night. I ran down from the second floor and saw him shaking uncontrollably, screaming at the top of his lungs. That was when I realized he had been dealt a monstrous blow that would dramatically affect our family and ultimately change him forever. It was a day that turned my life upside down.

The hatred Talal had towards his sister grew intensely, more than I could ever have imagined. Feelings of despair and shame consumed him. He quit his government job and stayed home for a long time. He felt ashamed and threw himself into despair. I became his punching bag every time he remembered what had happened. The humiliation he felt never stopped. He felt that his honor was lost in my eyes. I remember spending the days quietly, only for him to start drinking when darkness set in. He would turn into a vicious monster wanting to destroy everything around him. I spent those nights praying to God for them to pass peacefully.

This incident brought Talal's inner distrust of women to the surface. It caused him to lose confidence in himself and those around him, turning him into a hater. He started to feel that women were only capable of deceit, and that no woman was worthy of trust, not even his own mother. Did she not deceive him when she promised she would travel with him to England to study, only to leave him at the airport to venture out on his own? His sister, whom he had always seen as an angel with a kind demeanor, seemed to have stabbed him in the back, damaging his good standing in the community. He believed he was bad image for everyone to see. After that, could any woman ever be worthy of his trust? No one could!

In the days that followed, I made sure the children did not leave their rooms at night no matter what happened, and told them to call for help whenever I instructed them. As soon as the sun went down, Talal would start screaming and breaking things, thus scaring the children. The nights seemed like they would never end. I would be lying in bed wondering if he would hurt me at any moment. There would be screams, items breaking and threats but an apology would follow the next morning. This went on for years, until one day Talal was diagnosed with cancer. The cancer spread quickly. I can vividly recall his last moments. I would look at him, then glance at the children without saying a word. Just before he departed, I said, 'I forgive you.'

I was a queen one day, a sham queen, who got unseated from that phony throne and treated as a suspect. And here I am today, trying to get back on track with eyes that were kept in total darkness for years; eyes that weren't trained to see what they really wanted to see, but only what others wanted them to see."

THE PAINTING

Many of us may think that Wafa's circumstances are an isolated case of an aristocratic woman who married an aristocratic man. However, the reality is not that far from what happens to women from all classes. The previous story, with all the pain and suffering, gives us just one example of what really happens to women most of the time. If I were to describe this reality I would call it "A Painting in a Man's Exhibit," since in this situation, the woman is treated like property by the man, and he handles it as he pleases. Sometimes it is just an ordinary painting that meets requirements of the social mores. And sometimes it is the painting of a queen in her king's exuberant palace, a painting that wouldn't better her situation or change it even if it were real.

Wafa's story is no different from Maryam's, the country girl who lived the simple life and was married off against her will to her cousin. For her life too, was as good as dead. Both women experienced a lot of trouble in dire situations. They chose to keep silent and remain weak to keep their families intact; that way those on the outside wouldn't know the walls were cracking on the inside. Perhaps they were preserving what was left of their pride. Wafa' and Maryam's lives were like two paintings side by side on a wall in the middle of a house. The only difference between them was the type and color of the frame.

PALACE OF BONDAGE

The famous Arab poet, the late Nizar Qabbani, wrote:
"How can I liberate a woman who beautifies herself with bondage and who thinks her shackles are gold bracelets clanking on her wrist? How can I liberate a woman standing in line, in front of Shahrayar's bedroom, waiting for her turn?"

Talal is a good example of the controlling Arab man who wanted his beloved queen seated on the throne in front of him where he was the only one who could view her. It was obvious that money gave him the advantage to be very powerful and influential. Wafa', however, loved her jailer so passionately. She drew pleasure from making him jealous and igniting the spark in him every time he saw that she resembled the woman he painted in his imagination. She didn't pay much attention to her own needs. All she could do was wait for her role every morning to become a new Scheherazade to Shahryar, who enslaved her through the night. She loved her bondage as much as the other women. She even took delight in that bondage, ignoring the reality that as each day went by, a part of her persona vanished.

Wafa' saw herself in the eyes of her husband, in the eyes of society, and in the eyes of women around her. Never once did she look at herself with her own eyes. She did not believe that she even had the right to do so. She allowed societal codes to dictate her destiny.

Many may reject such realities, others may deny it. However, we have to admit that there are men who still to this very minute treat women the same way Talal treated Wafa'. Some of them may seek to "tame their horse" without any consideration for the horse's needs. The Eastern man sees his wife as if she were born only to please him. He loves to see her dressed up as he desires. Consciously or subconsciously, the Eastern man is happy to tighten his grip on her world to shape it according to his desires. To him, that is Manhood!

THE HONEYMOON IS OVER

After the honeymoon is over, and the couple is back home, life starts taking the shape that was formed by their union, and by that promise of walking the journey of happy marriage together. Their journey may seem as if it would be a wonderful beginning to fulfilling many dreams wrapped in a bright future. However, reality sets in, things change, and those masks of kindness that were put on during the engagement period start to fall off. Sameh no longer remains the one Rania knew; the loving fiancé who promised to let her finish her education, get a car, and work with him in the company. He no longer remains the man who promised her that they would socialize and strengthen relations within a high-level network of family and acquaintances. Those were only dreams and promises that ended before they celebrated their first anniversary. It was in that kneel where Wafa' paid the price. The kneel, where every man is in front of the girl of his dreams, later transforms into a tool to satisfy his desires and the object of his dominance.

Questions arise here: What caused this disappointment? How can the woman who is half of humanity's population, and is essential for life's balance, becomes a painting in a man's exhibit? Undoubtedly, we are not talking about all men here. I'm a firm believer that people are different, and not all men own exhibits in which to hang portraits of their women.

I would like to go back to my specific point of view on marriage; this mighty venture where a partner should be chosen based on transparency, clarity, and honesty between a couple. This is the basis of the healthy society we all aspire to live within. There is no doubt that the most important virtue at the beginning of the road is honesty, because there is no road that is devoid of thorns and stumbling blocks. But everything that is built on falsehood is vain. Frankly I say, that when a man marries a woman whom he does not love, or out of lust, or even to fulfill the wishes of his family, that marriage won't last! Even if it did, it would be absent of soul and warmth. Why is that? Because the man did not give himself the chance to explore the essence of the human part of his wife and did not give himself the chance to be filled with passion and did not satisfy her soul with his love.

Would that man view marriage as a life experience where he is equal to his companion? Or does he view it as an ownership, an object to be added to his possessions, which he can boast about? What makes a man view marriage in this unbalanced fashion? How can a woman accept that? What happens to the family? These questions are worth thinking about. We will be attempting to answer them in the following pages.

A WOMEN WITHOUT FEELINGS, OR A WOMAN WITH A SHAKEN IDENTITY?

Discussing the stereotypical image of the woman that is drawn by society according to its wants and needs compared to how her image reflects her true self, leads us to talk about the hidden feelings of the woman, and whether she is portraying her true self or portraying a distorted image that society prefers to see. Distorted images would certainly have an effect on the family and society as a whole. I can state here that we, the women, have contributed subconsciously to the shaping of the man's power and authority by seeking a protector, not because we are weak, but because we don't want the image of the "king" that we saw in our families' homes to be shaken in the image of our own husbands. I want to see the same power in my husband as my mother saw in my father whom she loved. I want him to protect me when I'm in danger and to stand beside me when I need him. This is how we were brought up and how we are expected to live. And things get even more complicated when we pass the "prestige of the king's image" to our daughters' minds as well.

In the same context, we can noticeably see the ability of a woman to ignore her feelings to take care of others, both physically and psychologically. I don't know exactly why women become disconnected from their true feelings. Is it caused by harsh life situations? Or is it because we choose the easier path to escape confrontation? What we see today is a façade of a woman who is dead inside, but skillful in making sense of everything else that goes on around her. She can talk consciously about raising her children and taking care of her husband, and those never-ending demands of the family. She can also talk about the worries of her endless work. However, she becomes shrouded in silence when she needs to talk about what goes on inside of her, or what haunts her existence, an existence hidden by her other half. It is that "other half" who is supposed to complete her, instead of repainting her whole image. To be fair, we cannot blame men totally for that. Women play a big role in maintaining these mindsets as well.

By going back to the root of the problem, we can see that the woman is the one who instilled in her son the belief that he is the "king" of the house, raising him to become a man who expresses his feelings and his anger rather easily.

We have raised our male offspring to be independent, confrontational, and to be able to defend themselves. Therefore, we do not fear for them if they get in trouble.

On the other hand, we are content with just worrying about girls as the weaker sex, paying little attention to empowering them and caring about their feelings. They are "girls till death" according to the popular saying. We did not teach them the same values we taught our sons. Instead, we teach them that they are in need of protection and that they are not capable of defending themselves.

We encouraged our sons to succeed and seek excellence, and at the same time, convinced our daughters that regardless of education and professional excellence, the ultimate goal is still marriage. To add insult to injury, we ignored their feelings and demands. We prevented them from expressing their true feelings when they were children, ultimately making them accepting of their husbands' disregard towards them, while giving little attention to themselves.

For example, if a girl fell in love with the neighbor's son, the family may reject him for reasons they deem logical. Then they may marry her off later to someone for other reasons they deem more logical and in her best interest. No wonder the wife can hide her feelings from her husband in the bedroom, for she is unable to even confess what she wants; to make love or not. While this is supposed to be a sacred and mutual relationship, it is only one-sided. One side expresses their physical needs and desires, while the other fears being viewed as rude. Add to that the feeling of shame. The upbringing process hinders the wife's transition from shyness to boldness. It also hinders the acceptance of the other, as well as expressing feelings and desire. The man's indifference to his wife's feelings and desires, since he is the stronger and more powerful male, makes the tough situation even tougher, especially if his upbringing instills in him this attitude, whether consciously or subconsciously.

Let's examine this matter more closely. Every one of us needs love and compassion, but there are many women who are deprived of these needs. Most of their psychological needs are left unfulfilled; while some of their physical needs are as well. If on a daily basis, a man treated the woman as a piece of furniture, or a painting, then that would translate into a marital relationship where he would have sex with his wife without touching her soul, devoid of her needs and desires, not wanting to know her or hear her. He wants to make love to a robot, or to satisfy a desire, not as part of a union and reciprocal passion with another as love is meant to be.

This type of man does not realize that power and control have nothing to do with it, especially when it comes to love making. It has to come spontaneously from the depth of the woman's soul, and at her benevolent free will. Only then would the true meaning of a union and it's beauty become prevalent, in order that the beauty of giving and interaction from the woman toward her husband would be part of the love-making experience. They could then share their humanity and discover areas of harmony that they probably never imagined. They could share a happiness that would unify them.

The nature of experiences the man goes through, as well as the social environment he grew up in, wastes an enormous potential for communication, balance, and true lifelong happiness. He would be treating those around him based on those experiences. How he treats his future wife would also be attributed to those experiences. As a child, he watched his father treat his mother with cruelty and heartlessness, and when he saw that type of behavior reoccur in other homes, he took that behavior as an example to follow, repeating the same sad past.

I cannot find better suited words that uncover the most important element in preserving the marital relationship -which is the foundation of our spiritual and social structure- than those of Gibran Khalil Gibran:

"Miserable is the woman who arises from the inattentiveness and restlessness of youth and finds herself in the home of a man showering her with his glittering gold and precious gifts and according her all the honors and grace of lavish entertainment but unable to satisfy her soul with the heavenly wine which God pours from the eyes of a man into the heart of a woman."

WHAT'S NEXT?

A man's neglect of the woman has a negative affect on most marriages. It is a global and many-faceted problem. This social epidemic is spreading quickly. In order to achieve peace and stability, we have to look upon each other with compassion, rather than self-centeredness. In spite of inevitable conflicts, psychological stability, attraction, and complementary relationships between the man and the woman are the secret behind a stable marriage. If mutual respect, trust, and fidelity rule over the marital relationship then nothing can shake a solid foundation of love.

Although we recognize what the root of the problems are, and what the solution is, we don't seem to be seriously constructing a new more enlightened method of education. I wish that every woman could see the reality of the life she is actually living and be raised up using new technology and foreign ideas. I also wish that every man would take off his dark shades and replace them with new, clear ones to see the woman in all the spectra of life.

She is not a lump of clay to be constantly punched down and conformed into one shape. We have to remember that clay is fragile.

We don't want this century to move on, while shuttling the woman's matters around from one hand to the other, and promising change -only to be in reality deceiving her. We in the Middle East must take pause to ponder what is happening all around us and shoulder the responsibility for change.

We mothers and fathers have to realize that attending to a girl's feelings is just as important as tending to the needs of a boy. Both of them will be shaping our society of the future. Both of them are responsible for constructing a healthy family capable of understanding and starting a constructive dialogue without being fearful of discussing any subject. That means that we have to denounce the notion of shame and the woman's weakness, especially those acts that were constructed with faulty methods.

The advice here is that we should teach the girl at an early age and then later as a woman, that she is of terrific value, and that no one owns her. That knowledge in return, would reinforce the woman's self-confidence and her belief in her capability to achieve success in life. We also must teach boys at an early age that girls are their partners, and that they both share the responsibility of living together in society. The girl should be given the freedom to express her opinions at home and at school, then later in the workplace and in society's institutions and legislative commissions.

Our archaic attitudes caused us to treat man's every whim as needs. We see woman's desires as restrictions. We tossed out women's feelings because of these customs.

It is absolutely necessary to change our cultural, societal, familial, and even religious discourse concerning women. A new realistic image of women should be created, one that is more just and humane. This can be achieved with education and modernization of the curricula to be compatible with new insight. This change should also come from the pulpit.

When I visited the museum of the Lebanese litterateur Gibran Khalil Gibran, a wonderful painting caught my attention. It was a painting of a woman embracing a man as he stood on the edge of a steep canyon, holding him around the waist from the back with her arms. What a magnificent painting of a creative artist who summed up his vision to reveal to us the wonderful and important role of the woman in guarding and protecting the man, making the world safer, as "it is not good for 'Adam' to be alone."

What does man want? The normal man wants a helpful, truthful, and content woman who would be a faithful wife and lover to cherish. He should treat her equally without fear or exaggerated guardianship. He should give her the best chance to express her feelings normally.

If the woman had been given the chance from the beginning to fulfill her potential and wasn't treated as a precious object that was easy to scratch or break, she would not need to hide her feelings and deny them. Her life would have been easier for her, her husband and the rest of her family. Children soak up their parent's balanced and sound feelings or pick up on their contradictions and suppression.

The marital relationship needs simplicity. If we are able to identify the points of weakness, then we can diagnose the situation and find the cure. A well-balanced marriage cannot survive without respect, compassion, and true love. There are many serious consequences if honest feelings and mutual respect are lacking and openness becomes non-existent.

When problems aren't tackled with a loving spirit that aims to preserve the cohesiveness and unity of the family, such disconnect reflects negatively on the children. Both husband and wife must put an effort into showing compassion and respect toward each other, paving the way for overcoming differences. Even a little compromise from each of them would be beneficial for the couple and for the family as a whole.

Finally, a responsibility lies also on the shoulders of the woman to realize her gifts, talents and potential. She has a role to raise a generation of girls who will not be subjected to the suppression and oppression that she endured, and to encourage rejecting all forms of oppressive authority.

Let me tell you what happened with my sister after graduation from high school. My sister loved languages and excelled in that field. She wanted to enroll in the College of Literature at university to study what she loved. However, my family pressured her to study business administration because they felt that would be a better suit for her. So, she yielded to their demands and studied business administration. Her love for languages never went cold, so as soon as she became employed, she financed her study of language. That effort later helped her move up the work ladder, giving her great fulfillment on her own terms.

The above picture is a matter that pertains to the whole of society, both individuals and establishments. Running away from our problems only increases rather than diminishes them. If we admit that there is a problem and we identify the reasons and discuss solutions, then we can begin to build a sound society that does not deny it's problems, but rather, seek to overcome them. That is how we must begin, for a journey of one thousand miles starts with a single step.

IS IT TO BE DEATH OR
A MISERABLE LIFE?

PAINFUL STORIES

The heart bleeds and the conscience aches at the countless stories of violence against women in Arab society. Some stories have secrets that never come to light. A murder hides under the guise of punishment, and revenge for honor. These cultural norms that are locked in stone become an integral part of immensely offensive practices against humanity.

Asma' was murdered at the age of twenty-eight. Her supposed crime was mutual admiration between her male Muslim neighbor and herself. As soon as her family learned of the matter, her father and her two brothers, Yousef and Jiryes, concocted a plan to protect the family honor. On a beautiful summer day, the brothers carried through with their plan by stabbing Asma' twenty-one times in order to kill her. Then they turned themselves in to police and were sentenced to only two years in prison. When they were released they both continued on with their lives by marrying and starting families as if the murder of their sister had never occurred. As for Asma's father, he died with the satisfaction of knowing his family shame had been removed, while in fact, it was the life of his daughter that had been removed from existence. His illiterate wife gave up on the life of her beloved daughter whose fate she helplessly watched unfold. What a stiff punishment for admiration only!

Amal was married for eleven years. She and her children suffered physical and psychological abuse from her husband during this time. There was no apparent reason for her offenses other than that Amal watched TV, arrived late for work and the children were disobedient. Amal never revealed this abuse to her parents. She did not want to dismay her ailing father. Because she suppressed this pain and suffering for years, she suffered a brain aneurism in her thirties. Through God's mercy, this incident did not remain a permanent physical problem.

Since Amal felt the need to end this unjust behavior, she took her children and fled. She worked two jobs in order to be able to provide her family with food, shelter and schooling. There had been no available deterrent to her husband's violence toward the family. Even the church could not protect Amal. She did not file any complaint against him, even though he failed to pay the support that was ordered by the court. After seven years of judicial and ecclesiastical court hearings, she was finally able to get a divorce, but at what price? One look at her children's poor behavior was enough to shed light on her broken family. She is still fighting to obtain freedom from the brunt of this violence against her family.

At the age of fourteen, Warda was repeatedly raped for three days. This incident fueled outrage and protest on social media. In April 2012, the court ruled that she should marry her rapist and her family was forced to agree. She suffered even more injustice at the hands of the media. Reports and opinions focused on the criminal alone and almost justified his heinous crime. The advice for Warda was to just forget the incident, without any regard to the fact that she was a woman who had just suffered an extreme act of sexual assault upon her person.

This horrific occurrence seemed to have skipped their conscienceless minds. Not only that, she was forced to marry the rapist and remain in that sick relationship for at least five years, after which he would be free to divorce her if he wished. "Rape and get married for free!" became a slogan that mocked the Jordanian judicial system; a system that is expected to defend the oppressed and to rule justly and equally to benefit both parties. We must find a permanent solution to these abuses and not affirm this offensive behavior through customs and an unfair judicial system.

A PERVASIVE PHENOMENON IN EVERY HOUSEHOLD

Violence is the masked thief who lives in many households in our Arab world, stealing the unity of the family little by little, wiping the smiles from faces. How is this happening and where has "the Arabic Spring" taken us with this violence?

As we have seen in these previous stories, violence causes turmoil in our homes and in our society at large. Who are the victims most of the time? Unfortunately, they are women and children. And in some cases, male-driven rampage causes the frustration of women to turn from being a victim themselves to becoming a perpetrator of this same violence against their own children, especially girls.

Mona Rishmawi of The Office of the United Nations High Commission for Human Rights (OHCHR) states, "Violence against women is one of the biggest societal ailments of our times. It is shameful that many women and girls who take a stroll down the street or go to work, or even those who stay at home, face painful experiences. When women and girls do not feel safe, then, half of humanity is not safe."

What is most noticeable is that domestic violence is not limited to low-income individuals and families. Many homes of wealthy families are also filled with physical and verbal abuse, as we saw in Wafa's instance. Violence against women and children, whether caused by religious or social motivation, has become a problem of alarming dimensions because it is so widespread throughout the Arab world. It is an open wound left to bleed profusely with no solution for healing.

IDENTIFICATION AND FACTS
The topic of this violence against women has been addressed by the United Nations, which resulted in the 1993 Declaration on the Elimination of Violence Against Women (DEVAW). This declaration recognized the urgent need for women to be granted legal rights. The link is: http://www.ohchr.org/AR/ProfessionalInterest/Pages/Violence AgainstWomen.aspx

Studies show that 20%-50% of women suffer violence at the hands of their husbands and other family members. Why not, since a lot of men consider women property and make them feel worthless? Such statistics prompt us to stop and take a look at the reasons behind such shocking results.

Many field studies for NGOs show that at least one out of three women face beatings, coercion and insults. The World Health Organization states that almost 70 percent of female victims are murdered by male friends. And according to United Nations Secretary-General, Antonio Guterres, women and children represent 80 percent of those who are killed and wounded by sharp weapons and firearms.

The problem here surpasses preserving the reputation and honor of the family. It is customary for men to reveal their oppression against women. Let's take for example what happens in times of war. When a man becomes oppressed, he exploits women to put stress on his male foes instead of fighting for revenge. This attempt to humiliate the enemy in this way is tied to the attitude of regarding women as the property of men, property which the enemy may use as he pleases. Thus our society with its oppressive laws against women ignores such acts.

FORMS OF VIOLENCE

During my work with women over a period of many years, especially young girls, I found that most were not even aware that they were being abused; and if they were aware, hid it from others. These signs were the most important factor in giving me the motivation to work on increasing awareness in women in order for them to realize that these abuses perpetrated upon them and the subsequent emotional injury come through no fault of their own. Every woman, regardless of her age or social status, has to recognize that this thief is intent upon stealing her soul, spirit and body, without comprehension by her whatsoever. The types of abuse we see are as follows:

Physical abuse: Deliberately using physical force against others to hurt and cause grave harm. Burning, kicking, beating with hands or objects, pushing, punching, breaking bones, and strangulation are the methods. Deprivation of basic needs such as sleep, food, drink, and shelter also fall within this type of abuse.

Sexual abuse: Sexual contact through force or coercion and pressure to engage in watching pornography. It also includes rape, sexual harassment, becoming the target of unwanted sexual comments as well as the abuse of authority to participate in sexual acts that conflict with both religious and moral rules.

Psychological and Mental Abuse: Any act or verbal aggression that threatens the woman's feelings, sense of self-worth, or her ability to control her own life. Intimidation, humiliation, belittling, name-calling, deprivation, accusations, shouting, and doubt of oneself could all result in various levels of inferiority, depression, and anxiety.

Financial abuse: This is the most widespread and pressing form of abuse in our Arab society. Women are not able to own property or receive inheritances. Working women carry family real estate debt but do not benefit from it's future value. They also get paid less for the same position occupied by a man and most families do not allow women to work even if they are educated and qualified. If the woman works, she is not given the liberty to make her own decisions. These women can be exploited and prevented from remarrying.

When a woman initiates a divorce, she loses all that is rightfully hers and must waive her right to spousal support to free herself from a failing marriage.

Social abuse: Is an act that deprives women of their rights such as isolation from society through severance of their communication with others – through legitimate social or familial methods.

REASONS FOR VIOLENCE

Violence is a global phenomenon that is spread throughout the whole social spectrum. Neither education nor financial status limits the practice of violence against individuals or communities. So why does violence exist in our environment? And why are women explicitly abused in our Arab World?

If the cause of violence could be diminished, it would be possible for this disease to decrease. I concur with Dr. Muhammad al-Khasawnah's view of violence which he addresses in his article entitled, "Violence: Its Causes and How to Treat It." (To see the entire article, please visit the website cited on the chapter's reference page.)

Violence within the family: May involve physical beating, name-calling and the demeaning use of words. This abuse may be perpetrated by the abuser and those being abused, as the abused individual searches for a place outside the home to vent his frustrations.

Feelings of inferiority: These may be due to poverty and lack of social potential, which encourage the individual to constantly compare himself to others, searching for ways to receive attention and positive affirmation.

Lack of proper discipline: The family in this current age does not have enough time to raise children by following healthy educational methods based on sharing and self-acceptance, as well as teaching tolerance of the mental, religious and financial situations of others.

Media: One of the strongest and most dangerous causes of abuse, especially programs that encourage revenge, killing, deception, and prostitution; whereas programs that encourage an entrepreneurial spirit, altruism or volunteerism are lacking. Even some national songs encourage tribal intolerance.

Unemployment: One of the reasons for violence. Economic disparity might lead to violence due to envy and deprivation. Feelings of injustice may cause violence and protests, and thus cause a rise in the crime rate.

Religious fanaticism: A distorted understanding of religion, and the appearance of extreme religious participation play a significant role in promoting and perpetrating violence, since such actions are considered obedience to God's will. The Arab Spring, blooming with goodness, spreading the spirit of love and forgiveness on the earth, is no longer the goal to which Arabs aspire. This religious extremism leads to murder. It has soaked the Arab lands with the blood of martyrs and transformed innocence to ignorance, stupidity, and lack of intellectual insight.

Tyranny and political oppression, lack of security, armed conflicts, and war: All these things carry within them nothing but pain, death, suffering, homelessness, fear, loss of family and humiliation. Time cannot heal these wounds but instead creates the desire for even more violence.

Tribalism and Arab pride create a constant conflict in familial societies: Tribal customs override rules and laws create pressure on society, especially the youth. They resort to violence in order to save face and protect the family's name.

WHY DOES A WOMAN SURRENDER TO VIOLENCE?
Mary wept so much that tears ran down her cheeks like water. She was overwhelmed with the countless images and questions that were plaguing her mind. A tape constantly played of painful memories and wounds, followed by fatwas and justifications. She did not want these scenarios to come to the surface, for she did not wish to appear naked when in reality she was clothed and strong-willed. She was sure she could withstand years of abuse and violence in order to be cloaked merely with the outward honor that was important in her society - a society that produced ugliness from every thing of beauty. "I have to endure this...my children are more important than me...what about my father's image, and what about my family? A virtuous woman keeps her secrets inside, and she endures the pain." Then she would remember her mother asking her what was wrong and she would ponder the amount of pain that she could suffer and the guilt she would feel from blaming herself for her circumstances.

This kind of disruptive dialogue was something Mary had become accustomed to which also grew more oppressive with time.

Even if she thought about breaking away into a world of freedom and healing, her thoughts would hold her back and convince her to sit calmly with a brave face showing only to the world outside.

Mary could no longer think of herself or her worth. She began to seek other types of expression but she had thought of her death and nothing else for a while even though attempting to create a new life with those whom she loved. She was invested in the lives of her children and hope for a brighter future.

This role was the source of her strength and the reason for her perseverance. Her limited financial resources prevented her from breaking away from this prison. She had also foolishly let her feelings be known to her neighbor and lost all that was precious along with any hope for a better future. Was there nobody who would listen or understand the agony of her soul and provide answers to change her situation?

So here is Mary, all grown up and married with children, the source of her pride, but her anxiety disorder persists. She doesn't know why she is so anxious or even want to know. She cries over the silliest of reasons, becomes angry and screams at others over even simple things. Depression has taken over, stealing her every joy and maintaining both physical and mental strength is hard. She cannot trust anybody. Would anyone even want to be intimately close to her? She is the strongest one against the cruel wind, and she is in better shape than the others, even advising the abused.

She had erected mighty forts where she hid her deep emotional wounds and secrets. Would she surrender? Would she drop that "Do Not Come Close" attitude that had been hers for so long?

We are standing here looking at the many forms of abuse and the daily challenges every woman faces, which cause her to live in a constant state of anxiety. She surrenders to violence, thinking that denial will cause it to disappear.

For example, we have a woman in her thirties, married with two boys, who has suffered societal, sexual, and physiological abuse as a child from a family member or a friend. She cannot control her feelings. She bursts into tears for the silliest of reasons and becomes angry and shouts over simple things. Even though depressed, she tries to act normal and comfort those who are abused but will not allow anyone to become close to her. Turmoil is buried deeply inside her soul and constant anxiety is an integral part of her life.

Women may hide behind this curtain of denial because the act of confronting abuse may end with a loss which would only be magnified if the case reached the legal systems that have been proven to present an unjust bias toward the abuse of women.

There is also an "unwritten silence" law in the Arab world that both the woman and her guardian practice. Rather than a denial of violence, there is an understanding of how violence against a woman should be handled. Bruises that appear on a woman's body are referred to as the result of "falling down the stairs" and she stays inside her house in order to hide them. This act leaves her feeling ashamed and guilty. Because of pressure placed on doctors to conform to this unwritten code of behavior, suicide is often filed under "extreme poisoning."

In the same context, the behavior of a woman who speaks out is portrayed as a deviation from societal norms, and the silence of other women in a similar situation is considered to be a virtue. There is a high price for a woman to pay for speaking up about violence because the cost may be the loss of custody of her children, or even the loss of her life. When a woman considers all the possible outcomes to her allegations of violence against her, she chooses silence and the cloak of honor. She decides to go on with her lonely suffering and losing her case already in her mind. Isn't that what we have learned from the society of shame; that all there is to worry about is the reputation of husband and family?

HONOR KILLINGS AND THE CONSEQUENCES

It is referred to as an honor killing to distinguish it from other murders by tying the "crime' together with the supposed offense claimed by the murderers. Honor crimes are the worst of all crimes because the murderer is the hero who avenges the family's honor.

It is known that our Arab society has the highest rate of honor killings in the world. Many times, the woman is killed by male siblings in order to remove her so that they might receive a larger portion of the inheritance. Most of the time, the perpetrator is the youngest brother because juveniles can only be sentenced to a period of seven years. The saddest thing about this type of situation is that the mother may agree to the violence or even worse, join in on the killing since she is the one who holds the highest status of guardianship of the family honor.

The use of honor killings also extends to the choices a woman makes in marriage; for instance, marrying someone of a different religion, sect, tribe or even one whom the family doesn't approve of. A woman can also be killed for having sexual intercourse with a man before marriage, for falling in love, or even for being seen with a man. The perpetration of an honor killing by a family member serves as a bold, wordless apology to the community and proves that there is no longer a cause for rejection of the family by its oppressive Arab society.

Nawal Sukkar, a Jordanian parliament member and activist, commented on a study done by Jordanian social specialists within a sample group of 2,000 Jordanian women. She shared that the study concluded that 97 percent of these women were abused. Another survey by researchers at Britain's Cambridge University showed that 35 percent of Jordanian teenagers believe that honor killings are justified. Their reasoning follows article 98 of the penal code Honor Crimes Under Jordanian Law, which states: "He who commits a crime out of extreme rage towards an unlawful and dangerous act committed by the victim, benefits from a reduction in the penalty."

The Jordanian Parliament refuses to repeal this article due to the religious and tribal support it has gained. Sukkar also mentioned that Jordanian Interior Ministry reports showed 82 female murders in 2013. One-fourth of these murders were classified under "honor killings." The 2014 Jordanian Human Rights Report indicated that ten percent of women and girls were murdered by male family members. The issue here is not the number of honor killings but the percentage of Jordanian males who support killing women for honor reasons.

Activist Hind Dalleh from the Women for Women Network in Lebanon said that there are over seventy court cases in Lebanon dealing with honor killings. The number of female victims in those cases was eighty-two. There are also killings that multiple males commit against individual women. How strange those twenty women were killed in mistaken identity cases! So, the fact that one-quarter of those women were mistakenly murdered leads us to think that there must have been some kind of recklessness in these women's lives. Dalleh added that 50 percent of the perpetrators were the husbands.

In Syria, civil rights activist Rabah (assumed name) said that talking about criminal offenses against females these days is considered a betrayal of all the women who are victimized due to the crisis in Syria even though she stressed that crime is crime, regardless of whether the reasons are criminal or political. She added that 300-350 female murders are registered in Syria every year with most of them being honor killings where the killer is not even punished thoroughly for the offense, thereby making these incomplete crimes.

We noticed that most of honor crimes are committed against girls who were involved in sexual relations before marriage. There is some support from doctors in Syria, Egypt, and Lebanon for these women and girls to have their hymens restored, giving them a chance to redeem themselves before the crime is discovered, especially if they were to be married soon.

RAPE

Nawal is a cleaning worker in a store in Eastern Amman. She regretted the day she accepted an overtime job to clean the owner's house. It was a trap he had set with the intent to rape her. Although the investigations proved her accusations to be truthful, Nawal could not obtain justice through the legal system. The rapist benefited from the controversial Article 308 in the Jordanian Penal Code. Once again, the law allows the rapist to avoid jail if he marries the victim and remains married to her for five years.

We can't even begin to scratch the surface when discussing rape. There is not much to be said about these girls in Jordan. Reports showed that of the 700 rape cases a year, 95 percent of the perpetrators avoided punishment.

Instead, the perpetrator gets rewarded for his crime by being gifted the girl in whole; and overnight she would become the property of the one who had victimized her. She has to obey him, and she cannot be asked about what has happened. She would also be denied a follow-up visit by a doctor. The law here answers to a society that only cares about "washing" the shame away. The shame here does not affect the offender as logic dictates, but rather the victim. The principle here is that honor is achieved at the expense of a woman's body and spirit.

It is vital that we realize here that the rapist does not commit his crime to satisfy a sexual desire or because he is attracted to the victim, but mostly because of the need to feel power and authority through controlling another person by sexual means.

We stand today against a painful situation that specifically utilizes the same culture to blame the Jordanian woman for her circumstances, since honor without care for her feelings is restricted to her virginity only.

The victim's rights now vanish in front of the judge since she is the guardian of the family's honor. Now that this honor is violated, a suitable solution must be found, or death will be her fate. So, which is better, being killed, or marrying her rapist? Either option benefits both the family and the rapist.

Let's imagine that a girl who is a minor is raped by a married man in his thirties or forties. How would that girl feel being wed to him, knowing her body is worthless and her feelings are condemned to a life in prison? How can she live with him while being raped day after day since she is legally and lawfully his? How can the rape victim, living in an environment that allows her no mercy and cannot forget what happened to her, be with a man who abuses and humiliates her in a society that practices murder in defense of an honor? Let us list the types of abuse that she endures: physical, sexual, societal, and psychological. As for the family, their daughter's fate is in their hands; that fate is either death or a miserable life.

WHAT IS THE SOLUTION?

This discussion and stories about violence against women could continue endlessly without progress because the custom and culture of shame are at the forefront, preventing positive change in our society.

So far, calls from the podium have not been successful in diminishing this daily violence that takes place in various forms in our Arab World. Perhaps some groups even use such places to instigate violence.

Since violence starts in the home, it must end in the home as well, because it is there that ideas about society are formed within the family unit. Hurting and bleeding souls can receive healing and restore hope in life. But change cannot be achieved if there is no personal conviction and willingness from women to stop all forms of violence against them.

There is no doubt that a comprehensive solution to discrimination and violence against women cannot happen without scrutinizing the reasons for violence, and educating parents and teachers on how to deal with the behavior of children and youth. It is essential to steer males away from cruelty and abuse, while instilling noble ideals and values and practicing faith and piety without prejudice. We also need a commitment to present role models of righteous forefathers. Too often, violence is passed down to boys by watching their fathers abuse their mothers and sisters, and thus these boys repeat the same offenses when they are married.

Although many Arab activists fight for women's rights and feminist discourse has spread through support organizations and alliances, there still is a stumbling-stone that blocks those efforts. It is the lack of cooperation between these different entities. Coordination among these organizations could lead us to eliminate the shortcomings of our culture and allow us to hold on to the positive attributes. This would allow women to stand together against the spread of shame, violence and faulty cultural habits of inferiority that have been previously passed on to their children.

We have mentioned that societal values in the Arab World affirm the transfer of authority from father to brother and from husband to son. This ritual keeps the woman a prisoner to male hegemony. However, governments are capable of lifting the immunity that the male enjoys within the family, and to not releasing him from personal accountability when he makes mistakes and commits violence against women. Governments need to enforce harsh punishment by treating such cases as criminal, wherein the perpetrator is punished without any exception.

I like the new Egyptian method of combating sexual harassment against women, be it at work or in the streets or anywhere else, through the recruitment of teams that specialize in confronting individuals who lack a moral and social conscience. The method is still new, but I think by monitoring these events, this method will succeed in Egypt regardless of the large population, unemployment, and poverty.

Governments must do all that is needed to make accountability happen. Also, individuals who control media and oversee educational curriculum must cease to use stereotypes to define women that humiliate and tarnish their image in society

The Turkish television series "Bab Al-Hara" and demoralization of women in commercials are two examples. The sexual allure of women should not be used for marketing products. They should not to be compared to immoral Western women in mind, clothing or belief. Media must stop putting so much pressure on young men -especially those ready to marry - by painting false portraits of women. Men need to see that there is a distinction between what they see on TV and what is real. These degrading portrayals of women reflect negatively on men's future decisions and thus how a husband treats his wife.

References
1. "Declaration on the Elimination of Violence Against Women 1993", The Reality of Violence against Women in Jordan - The National Council For Family Affairs, chapter 3 page 5.
2. Muna Rashmawi - Human Rights Office, United Nations. A Call To Action. Women, Religion, Violence, and Power - Jimmy Carter, page 132.
3. Free from Violence in the Family, Dr. Amparo Medina, page 19.
4. The National Council for Family Affairs Workshop, March 2008.
5. Shamkhy Jabr, "Violence Against Women", The Civilized Dialogue.
   http://www.ahewar.org/search/Dsearch.asp?nr=2282
6. http://www.ncfa.org.jo/Portals/0/VAW vision.pdf
7. Dr. Hayfa Abu Ghazaleh, Secretary General of the General Council of Family Affairs. Policies, Violence Against Women: A Collaborative Vision To Create Change Vol. 2 June/July 2008.
8. Muhammad Al-Khasawnah, "Violence: Its Causes and Methods of Treating It." Ajloun News Agency.
   http://www.ajlounnews.net/index.php?module=articles&category=90&id=8984.
9. Citizens and Family Health Census in Jordan 2012. Alrai Newspaper. Department of Census
   http://dos.gov.jo/dos_home_a/main/index.htm.
10. http://ar.wikipedia.org/wiki/
11. http://hunasotak.com
12. Female Murder is A Crime that Carries A Lenient Sentence in the Arab World.
   www.http://www.hespress.com/international/87325.html
13. http://www.watantimes.com/blog
14. http://www.ipetitions.com/petition/308_jordanian_law
15. http://www.arabic.irinnews.org/Report/4154/. Escaping- the Sexual Assault Sentence-In-Jordan
16. http://www.women.jo/ar/news_details.php?news_id=2653
17. http://www.7iber.com/2012/04/rape-and-marry/
18. http://jordantimes.com/projected-penal-code-amendment-scraps-article-pardoning-rapists-who-marry-victims
19. http://www.ipsinternational.org/arabic/nota_txt.asp?idnews=1820
20. http://www.maghress.com/alalam/51818
21. http://www.miftah.org/publications/books/violence_against_women_in_palestinian_society.pdf
22. http://www.amnesty.org/ar/annual-report/2013
23. http://www.shura.bh/1

Ali Abdullah Al-Aradi, A paper on Financial Violence Against the Family.

24. http://www.ohchr.org/AR/ProfessionalInterest/Pages/Violen ceAgainstWomen.aspx

CONFLICT BETWEEN EMPLOYER EXPECTATIONS VERSUS FAMILY DEMANDS

INEVITABLE FATE

Nada is in her twenties. She has an angelic smile and a childlike face in spite of the extreme emotional turmoil lingering in her soul. Her mother divorced when she was only four years old. Because her father did not want his wife to have custody of the six children, Nada grew up yearning to live with her mother and longing every day for a hug. Her father remarried a year after the divorce and the stepmother treated Nada and her siblings kindly, hoping her husband would not divorce her as well.

Nada grew up in a small village with separate schools for girls and boys. Her only forms of entertainment were doing household chores and occasionally visiting with cousins. She was the eldest daughter, older than Mahmoud and Yousef, but younger than Ahmad the eldest. Only Anoud and Shurooq did not attend school since they were less than five years of age.

Often, Nada would stand by the window overlooking the main street of her village. She would watch the pedestrians hoping that she'd be allowed to leave the house without a chaperone just like her brothers. She would gaze at the sky watching the birds and wishing she could be the one flying toward the horizon. She let her daydreams run wild.

When Nada turned fifteen a young man from the neighboring village came to ask for her hand in marriage. She wasn't forced to marry him, but listening to the gossip of her brothers and relatives pierced her ears like a siren warning of inevitable danger if she didn't. It seemed best for her to accept this suitor. So she welcomed him not knowing anything that a marriage entailed and the responsibilities that came with it. How could she know, when she was still only a teenager attracted to whatever new thing came into her life?

She became engaged to Nasser at the beginning of summer and two months later they wed. A big celebration for them took place at one of the wedding halls. Nada was beautiful in her white dress, with green eyes and soft hair flowing down behind her veil. She was a very thoughtful girl, deciding to wear flat shoes so that Nasser wouldn't look so short beside her.

Nada was the first one to give the family a celebration. Relatives sang and danced for her all night long. She felt like she was the only person on the face of the earth, but she couldn't hide the sadness under her makeup. How could she be joyful when her mother was not with her to celebrate this special occasion?

After two and a half years of marriage, Nada returned to her father's house as a divorcee, crying over the loss of her twin boys whom she was forbidden to contact. Her siblings and stepmother were not happy with her return. Her father considered the divorce a shame that she had brought upon the family since Nada was obviously an unacceptable and disobedient wife.

Only because her dowry was returned was she accepted back into her father's home. Nada thought that divorce would be the beginning of freedom. She wanted to achieve the dreams she had wished for when she was a girl. She aspired to finish high school and get a college degree so she could work to earn money and help her boys later in their lives.

She constantly struggled to obtain custody of her boys, but faced opposition from her father who said, "I'm not going to support your boys! Isn't it enough that I have to support your siblings?"

The first month of her return home went by as if it had been a year. Her heart wouldn't be consoled and all her attempts to see her boys ended in failure. Eventually Nasser allowed her to see them only one day a month. He did not respect the custody laws and refused to give Nada custody of her twins. Since her father was not willing to support his grandchildren financially, she had no recourse to Nasser's harsh decision. Nada lived under the constant judgment of a failed marriage coming from both her father's family and the family of her in-laws.

Nada's future now seemed uncertain and she did not know what step to take next. Many questions went through her head: "Would my father let me go back to school, or should I ask him to let me work outside the house, or even outside the village? Maybe he will accept this idea if I give him my paycheck. Can I go to the city to work after facing so many closed doors?" Nada could not have foreseen the painful reality of her current situation.

And there were other questions that almost caused her to lose her mind: "Why me? Why did he divorce me? Who am I in this house? Who am I in this society? Why do they expect me to stay silent and not complain though I'm going through a bitter, tough situation? Why wouldn't my father treat me fairly when I owe nothing to him? I wish he would just listen to me! I wish his wife would accept me as a friend. Who understands me? Who feels my sorrow? Who can look inside me to see the shards of my heart that has been broken with humiliation and contempt? Woe to me for what has happened to me!"

It is evident that Nada's story reflects on several problems. Because my goal is to focus on the challenges that face the Arabic woman and her many roles in and outside of the home, I will try to address the root problem and how she reached such an unwanted ending, causing her to live in such uncertainty and disappointment.

We know that there are biological roles that are specific to women, which a man is not able to perform, such as bearing children and nurturing them to adulthood. There are also roles that a man performs which require more physical strength. These roles are called "gender roles" because they are related to "gender", the word that identifies a person as either male or female.

There is another role as well: expectations established by society for men and women outside the home. This role is closely tied to a culture's customs. Because of the Arab culture, unhealthy societal roles keep the relationship between the man and the woman in constant turmoil.

We see this take the form of positive correlation when the husband enhances the position of his wife and she becomes more productive and strengthens the family. The marital relationship may also take the form of inverse association each time a man oppresses his wife to keep her on an unequal footing. She becomes less productive, causing problems in the educational and familial areas.

In this day and age it is becoming critical for a wife to work and help support the family financially; but work outside the home causes a challenge for her, for she now needs her husband to assist with household chores. She would like him to clean, cook, buy groceries, help the kids study and oversee their activities, etc. These responsibilities were formerly those of the woman, but now they both must contribute so the woman may also excel and be promoted to available leadership positions. We see here that the man could use the broom and the sponge, while the woman would hammer the nail in the wall if they both stood united together against societal norms. But modern customs are destructive and unfair towards women.

The "working-woman's role" requires the husband to be more committed to the home so that the marital relationship may be successful. Thus a new social development that begins in the home could work it's way into the marketplace. A healthy marital relationship builds upon love, good intentions and unified sacrifice in order to keep the marriage sustained. However, social norms and customs contradict this approach and deem the man's help in the home an insult to his manhood; thereby calling for him to not cooperate with his wife in order to demonstrate his authority over her. In that case, there will always be a winner and a loser, instead of two unified winners who cooperate to achieve their best roles through equality, justice and respect. I am confident a unified approach by both husband and wife would change society's viewpoint; rather than being consumers people would become producers, innovators and life-givers.

We saw that Nada grew up in a very unhealthy physical, social, and psychological environment where there was no understanding of gender equality within her family, and this ultimately affected her marriage. When it ended in divorce, she found herself captive to the limitations that her father had imposed upon her because she was a female divorcee. She did not feel she had a role in or outside of the home except to obey her father's demands without argument. The idea of love and respect had become nonexistent and she had lost her desire to live.

UNFAIR PARTNERSHIP

Most of the time Arab culture sanctifies the woman's responsibilities towards her husband in the marital relationship, but does not sanctify the man's responsibilities toward his wife. Because of the current role of the wife and her lack of status in the institution of marriage, the Arab woman is constantly worried and insecure. She fears that she will find herself one day living outside of the institution, which provides her with only a minimum level of security. In the marital relationship, the weaker the woman, the more she is forced to respect her husband, rather than him protecting and appreciating her. What a contradiction!

If she leaves the marriage financially unfit and unable to make definitive decisions, she may end up like Nada, divorced, alone and separated from her children. This sudden independence caused by divorce places heavy financial, social, and psychological burdens on the woman.

The Western woman lives in an entirely different sociological system than that of the Arab woman. Her society respects who she is as a person regardless of whether she is divorced or married. The married Western woman isn't weak and she doesn't have to follow her husband's orders. She has freedom to state her opinions inside and outside of the home.

Let us now go back to the word "independence." Does the woman in our society truly have independence, whether in the home of her birth or the home of her husband; whether she is single, divorced, or married?

Most Arab women grow up prioritizing the needs of their families and children over their own. My Mother is one of those women, and had I not broken free of these inherited mental chains, I would also be following these unjust traditions. A woman's sense of responsibility does not end with raising children. She keeps on giving unconditionally, even with the grandchildren, finding value in the love they bestow upon her in return for her attention. I am by no means patronizing the noble role of wife, mother and grandmother, but I seek to expose the painful situation of women not allowing themselves the right to be dignified partners in the marital relationship. They have the right to the ownership of their bodies, and the right to nurture and protect them. Deep within these women are many hidden jewels and neglected talents, screaming to rise to the surface and touch reality. What we see instead, are not the fulfillment of dreams women have planned for themselves, rather predefined roles society has constructed for them.

THE PRICE OF CHOICE

Nada (whose story is at the beginning of this chapter) was denied an education as a young woman. Our next story is about a working woman who appears to have all the components of independence. She was given a choice in marriage, education, and work, but was she able to enjoy that independence? It is the story of a woman who is a dear friend of mine.

One day, I received a call from my friend Suzi. She said, "I want to ask for your advice on whether I should get a divorce." I was surprised and asked her what was going on, but when I heard how distraught she was, I insisted on seeing her in person. When we met, she told me details of her life; a story she had never told anyone, fearing embarrassment. Suzi had this to say:

"You know that my husband and I we were engaged for an extended period and I thought I knew him well. But even during that period, he didn't show any of the signs of who he really was until after the wedding. He was kind, courteous, and manly, but he turned into a monster after marriage. That's the truth! He abused me both physically and mentally.

Five years went by before I realized that his lack of self-confidence caused him to lose jobs, and I became the breadwinner of the family. He, on the other hand, controlled my life like he would control a car, using the steering wheel to take me wherever he wanted, stop whenever he wanted, park wherever he wanted. I was the one who had to keep up with his pace. Where is my dignity? Where is my will? And where is my femininity? How can I live the rest of my life with him? I no longer have any desire to stay married to him."

Suzi broke down telling me another story of her husband's mistreatment. She shared how he would force her to visit his family every day after returning from an exhausting day at work. He made her cook his meals though he did not work and was home all day. He would not lend a hand to help with anything. Suzi supported him, bearing the responsibility for their livelihood and if she dared to argue or disagree with him, it would result in mental or physical harm.

The issue here is more significant than one person's behavior. It is a phenomenon that affects women at every level of society, since she is not viewed as an equal partner in marriage. She does not possess the same rights as the man to make decisions and act independently

AN IRON WOMAN

When a woman asked to seek employment outside the home in the past, she faced rejection from her family as if that demand were not within her right. This dismissive attitude made it look like the culture did her a favor by supporting her. When she did work, society expected her to become an iron woman; a tool to be used when and where needed.

In the morning she could be a doctor in one of the hospitals, and upon returning home from work in the evening, she would assume the role of a housewife. She would be expected to perform both roles skillfully without asking for help; at least from her husband, her closest relative. I can say without hesitation that the position of the Arab woman today is based on need and demand. When the financial situation in the family is strong she will not need to go outside the home to work, even if she wanted to. On the other hand, when the financial situation requires that she work, she is expected to do that with no adjustments made for a new situation. Without forfeiting her role as a housewife, who then has the responsibility to meet the demands of the household?

To add to that hardship, a job vacancy might not even be available for a woman. Unemployment rates in the Arab world, especially among women, is very high as the statistics prepared by World Bank for 2013 show in this table below:

#	Country	% Of Women Unemployment
1	Jordan	22.1%
2	Lebanon	11%
3	Tunisia	15.5%
4	Egypt	29.3%
5	Somalia	7.4%
6	Yemen	38.8%
7	Saudi Arabia	80%
8	Palestine	50.6%

The chart above shows that the unemployment rate among women weakens the workforce. The Arab countries have the highest rate of women's unemployment in the world. Women represent 40 percent of the unemployed or 25 percent of the workforce.

"Feminizing unemployment" is a term used in the Arab marketplace. Even with these dwindling numbers, we all agree that the current situation in Arab society requires that the woman join the workforce; not because she loves working in a particular field, but rather to stand by her husband and help him meet their endless financial needs. I see that as fair, because we cannot put all the weight on the shoulders of one person, but it is only logical that the couple share responsibilities of home and family.

From another angle, the Arab culture must come together to find ways to release pressure on the family unit, such as European societies have done. Otherwise, outside employment for a woman can become a curse and a burden. She would have to choose between taking on a great deal of responsibility for which she cannot muster the energy, or chose to not work and devote herself to her household. If the current situation remains unchanged in our culture, then the most massive load would slide to one side of the boat (the woman's), leading to an imbalance. That type of boat keels over.

In Arab culture, the standard excuse for a lack of cooperation on the part of the husband is that he is the one who pays the dowry and incurs debt for the wedding; but reality says otherwise. The woman in many cases bears the cost for the wedding indirectly by paying off the debt afterward in servitude to her husband.

Opinions vary regarding the type of career a woman can choose, thus making it hard for the woman since she wouldn't even be able to decide if there is a need for her to work. That decision is either up to the father (who worries about his daughter's reputation in the workplace), or the husband who may not be pleased that his wife is employed in the same place as men.

We are still in a struggle between the man and the woman. Although women in the workforce have reached positions of great influence, they are still unable to obtain promotions like men due to workplace discrimination. Even if a woman reaches a better position at work, it wouldn't be without paying a hefty price. The cost for her could include additional work hours, more stress, or traveling on short notice.

As for how other women perceive the successful woman, we do not believe that a female doctor has the ability to be as skillful as her male counterpart. We do not trust her abilities to analyze critical matters, so we prefer to see a male doctor; erroneously thinking that he is better in dealing with patients, finding solutions, changing laws and resolving disputes, as well as managing money.

When a woman returns to work, she has to be perfect. She needs to be a skillful worker without any assistance, a companion and lover to her husband, and a compassionate mother. However, all these expectations can cause her stress, leading to chronic fatigue, boredom, and a desperation that reflects on all aspects of her life, including fracturing the emotional and sexual relationship with her husband.

Psychoanalyst Helen Dutch, who specializes in the study of practicing work and life balance, mentions in her work that full-time employment while raising small children are two things that cannot exist along with the physical and psychological balance of one human being. The woman who balances many different roles may suffer a mental struggle after expending a tremendous amount of energy toward two critical tasks; motherhood and work.

With this current social structure, splitting unequal roles between the husband and wife within the family hinders the woman's ability to balance the various tasks that she must perform.

A DIFFERENT TYPE OF CHALLENGE

In an article by Dima Mahbubah in the Al-Ghad Newspaper published May 3rd, 2012 titled, "Work and Family Pressures Are the Biggest Challenges the Modern Woman Faces, " Mahbubah describes the life of a high school teacher in one of the private schools who complained about the home environment that clouded her family and married life because of work pressure. The teacher said, "House chores pile up because my daylight hours are consumed with teaching and preparing for the next school day, which in turn negatively affects my family life and marriage."

The teacher stresses that she tries her best to avoid an unbalanced workload at home by organizing her time and splitting the chores between herself and her husband. They both fail because her husband also has a full workload. She mentions that stress from work not only affects her family relationships, but her interests and hobbies as well. She is unable to even socialize, except on her days off.

Sociologist Dr. Muhammad Juraybee' sees that designating a relative to care for children during work hours or enrolling children in a good daycare is a suitable solution. The working wife would then be able to separate her employment responsibilities from that of her family's in order to limit the number of marital problems that could cause a divorce situation. But what if this solution were not available, and what if there were no alternative?

The Jordanian Labor Law no. (8) of 1996 mandates that companies with more than twenty female married employees should provide a suitable place of care for employees' children of less than four years of age, provided that the number is not more than 10 children (Art. 72). However, this measure affects the decision to hire women in large establishments forcing women to accept work at smaller ones. Another option is that the woman leave the workforce altogether.

In an article published on May 26th, 2012 in the Al-Ghad Newspaper by Rania al-Sarayrah, the conflict of daycare centers was addressed. The topic, "Mothers Living in Constant Worry Due to Lack of Daycares at Their Workplace," details the working woman's struggle with the rising cost of living that forces her to be employed outside the home while raising her children. Her sacrifices, however, are not rewarded with help to accomplish both tasks.

The story instead discusses the hardships and challenges that face a working wife and mother named Dalia, who struggles with daycare problems; from the scarcity of daycare facilities to the facilities' distance from her work, to the high price of daycare enrollment. The alternative to bringing in a domestic worker becomes very difficult due to requests for higher wages.

Dania's situation mirrors that of many working mothers who are forced to leave a "mother-hostile environment" after delivering a child. Such matters are not treated with fairness.

Salam, another working mother, was also discriminated against in the workplace. All bonuses and other promotions were passed on to Salam's male colleague, although they both worked the same hours. No consideration was taken for Salam's strong job performance and the need to balance her employment responsibilities with time for her children. More importantly, her employer did not adhere to the laws that protect her rights such as maternity leave, breastfeeding hours, etc.

These are a few examples that reflect the reality of the working Arab woman and the challenges she faces in her roles as mother and employee, and the lack of appreciation and respect that is undeserved from society, and especially from within the family.

Society imposes firm hours of employment on the woman, just as it does on the man, but ignores the woman's additional role as a mother. Instead, she is accepted solely as an employee, and the culture refuses to treat her as a mother in the workplace.

I believe that equality begins when all supportive opinions and methods more readily allow women to work in a healthier environment. Accomplishing a positive balance involves respecting motherhood through providing daycare for the working woman's children, and having her weekly time-off coordinated with that of her husband and children. Just as the husband and wife are partners in working to provide income, they should also be partners in taking care of their children.

WHAT IS DESIRED AND WHAT IS REALITY
Society requires the woman today to be inhumanly perfect. She must be the employee, the educator, the mother, the sister, the friend, and the lover.

She must play all these roles without hesitation or objection. Arab culture has allowed the multiplication of the woman's duties under the pretext that she had asked to be equal to the man.

For change to occur, the current situation must be observed from both sides of the equation; the side of the woman and the side of society. If the woman asks her culture to defend her and acknowledge her as a complete being, she needs to first use her intelligence to recognize all her abilities from the correct viewpoint in order to expect the man's understanding and acceptance.

In other words, the woman has to respect her person and know her value before demanding her rights if they become violated. Ideally, we would like the woman to say, "I am important, and I can make a difference in my life and the lives of others." She should not accept marginalization, for freedom is gained not given. Simone De Beauvoir states, "If one wants freedom for one's self, he has to want it for others."

The liberation of women in our Arab society must first start with changing the rules that govern a woman's relationship with a man. Although there is no doubt that change is necessary, the change we are seeking is one that can become a reality in day-to-day practice in people's lives, where positive attitudes towards women become woven into the fabric of society. Only then can all roles and rights of the woman be recognized. Society could transform into one that nurtures healthy marriages through many different methods, including pre-marital counseling and family planning (ending abortion as a form of birth control). Awareness and protection of a woman's mental and physical health could be the result of these changes.

Change cannot be achieved through wishes alone. Promising young people who are willing to cooperate with one another to raise awareness of the need for change among all classes and sectors, could combine efforts to construct a social force to press for reform of the laws of justice for both sexes. This force could change the dominant system of culture that accepts tyranny, oppression and denies the rights of others. Surely the result would be to tilt our cultural makeup towards the overlooked virtues of forgiveness, love, and acceptance of others and their right to make personal individual choices.

These difficult tasks are assumed to be the primary responsibility of the Arab woman. But freedom comes with a hefty price that the liberated woman pays for with her health, peace of mind, and societal opposition. It is better for her to pay one price to be free than to pay another and remain a slave. Instead, she must use her intelligence to think of ways to effectively challenge discrimination in order to be able to make her own decisions. She also has to fight the belief that a man is to produce and the woman is to consume.

Marriage and the responsibilities that come with it are enough to make couples grow weary. When one partner grows distant from the other this weariness becomes massive. Let us rethink our decisions, thoughts, and aspirations before entering into marriage so that we can have the best relationship intended by God!

A SUCCESS STORY

Since the woman represents half of society, let that half be an impactful one to make a difference! The woman is surely fit to convey her message since she is the one who has endured real pain and suffering. She should steadfastly raise her head in pride and spread her message to the world!

Let us look at this true story told by my friend, Manar Al-Nimri. The story shares what can happen to women when society holds them back from success, and then how an opportunity can allow them to reveal their hidden talents and abilities:

Rafia is her name. She is a mother of four, and the second wife to an unemployed man. She finished fifth grade at her village school, and then dropped out since it was considered shameful to educate girls in those days. She spends her time at the tent washing, cooking, smoking and drinking tea. But Rafia's circumstances are about to change!

Barefoot College in India was founded in 1972, for the purpose of gathering women from various countries who were living in marginalized situations. These women were brought to India in order to provide them with an education and teach them life skills, thus enabling them to advance in their societies.

The founder of the college visited Rafia's village. The idea of being in the company of other women who had faced rejection appealed to Rafia. But how could she travel to another country when she wasn't allowed to go five meters away from the tent? She persisted because she did not want her four girls to face the same fate as herself. Approval was hard-won. Ultimately, she convinced her husband to let her travel with her friend Um Badr, who took her son along as a male companion to represent the family.

Rafia enjoyed learning how to generate electricity using solar energy. She took notes and memorized everything she learned about solar panels until her husband called to tell her he would divorce her if she didn't return home. Fearing she would lose her daughters, Rafia returned, but she had caught the vision of what women's education could help her accomplish and was able to convince her husband to let her return to India and rejoin the course. She successfully finished and returned home happy and hopeful that she would be able to help her village with her knowledge of how to implement this wonderful project. She persisted until she obtained a business loan. Then, she was able to generate electricity in her home, just after her husband had been sent to jail for smuggling.

Rafia encountered a further funding problem since the Ministry of Planning and International Cooperation in Jordan questioned the viability of the project. Instead, the Indian government helped by purchasing solar panels. Rafia then expanded the project to generate solar power for eighty houses in the northern desert of Jordan. She would have been able to provide more homes with solar power if only the government of Jordan had believed in her ability to use her new skill. Then the government would have been able to establish a school to teach the production of solar energy to other women in Jordan.

References

1. http://www.youtube.com/watch?v=O9qAV4v33FM2-
2. Costie Bandali, "Girl's Education and Woman's Horizons." Jarrous Press, Tripoli-Lebanon, 1998. Pages 97-99.
3. Dima Mahboubah, Al-Ghad Jordanian Newspaper, May 26 2012. "Work and Family Pressures Are the Biggest Challenges of the Modern Woman".
4. Rania Al-Sarayrah - Al-Ghad Jordanian Newspaper, May 26, 2012. "Mothers Worried About Lack of Daycare At Their Workplace".
5. Nawal El-Saadawi, "The Naked Face of Arab Women", The Arab Institute for Studies and Publishing, Beirut 1977, pages 164-165.
6. Costie Bandali, "Girl's Education and Woman's Horizons." Jarrous Press, Tripoli-Lebanon, 1998. Pages 97-99.
7. Jordan's Unemployment "Al-Madinah News", The Rising Numbers of Unemployment in Jordan. http://www.almadenahnews.com/article/251975-2013
8. Nawal El-Saadawi, "The Naked Face of Arab Women", The Arab Institute for Studies and Publishing, Beirut 1977, pages 164-165.
9. Unemployed Women in Saudi Arabia, 413506 http://www.albawaba.com/ar/80
10. UNESCWA annual report for 2013, "Survey of the Economic and Social Development in the Arab Region 2012-2013".
11. http://www.pp.ps/atemplate.php?id=6691
12. The Woman and The Family / 514243 Women Unemployment in Palestine 38-4 http://m.masralarabia.com
13. Dr. 'Abd-al-Mun'im Muhammad al-Tayyeb Hamad al-Neel, Unemployment in the Arab Countries: The Reality, Causes, and Solution Mechanisms (Complete Study), The High Institute for Financial and Banking Studies Khartum.
14. http://nabdapp.com/jump.php?id18363348

A WOMAN'S SHADOW

RAW'AH THE ACCUSED

Raw'ah is a twenty-two year old young lady who was molested in preschool at the young age of four. Her mother kept silent about the incident for fear of harming her daughter's reputation. During puberty, Raw'ah was again molested by her uncle and when her mother confronted the aunt, the child was accused of lying and immorality and the mother was forced out of the uncle's home. Raw'ah was outraged that her mother was afraid to tell her father and decided to retaliate by molesting her youngest cousin. Eventually, Raw'ah began to despise this ugly act and her guilt led her to believe that she was evil while everyone else was good. Poor Raw'ah had taken revenge for the inequities that she had been subjected to through no fault of her own.

Although Raw'ah was a beautiful young woman her parents criticized her appearance, hoping this would cause her to be humble and respectful. Consequently, Raw'ah became fearful and isolated herself from society. Raw'ah's father beat her whenever she disagreed with him and treated her as a male instead of a female because he believed her femininity brought dishonor upon him. As Raw'ah struggled with the pain of her early life, she wondered why she had not been born a man.

Raw'ah's father put pressure on her to marry but when she disapproved of his choices she became suicidal. Her parents had no idea that she spent hours on the Internet talking with strangers while they were content that she was at home under their supervision. She deceived her parents in order to have the freedom to be with her friends and even had thoughts of running away from home to pursue love and freedom.

Should Raw'ah's parents have been suspicious of her behavior and were the thoughts racing through her head a kind of oppression, or was she merely surrendering to her circumstances? Her story is real and took place in Egypt. Oppression becomes a woman's shadow that follows her wherever she goes, bringing her humiliation and disrespect merely because of the fact that she is female.

Almost 100% of Arab women are afflicted with this painful injustice. The oppression of women has become one of the most discussed issues of current Arab writers but does their work have any positive impact?

In this chapter, I will delve deeply into the reasons for this oppression and the many forms that it takes as I consider the various circumstances of the women outlined in previous chapters. The sociological viewpoints I put forth are the result of my many in-depth conversations with Dr. Maher Samuel, a physician, Christian scholar and psychologist whom I met in Jordan. Dr. Samuel also holds a Master's degree in Philosophy and Religion from Trinity University in the United States. He shared with me an overview of his studies on the oppression of women while I questioned him and gave my input as well.

THE MAIN FACTORS IN THE OPPRESSION OF WOMEN
First Factor: The current perception of women in the Arab world
Dr. Samuel states "in the Arab World, a deep-rooted conviction dominates people's minds that the woman lacks sound judgment and falls short of meeting standards set by religion." (TN: Naqisat 'Aql Wa Deen. Literally, having incomplete brain and religion.)

The unexpected problem is that this conviction creeps even into the minds of the enlightened. Most of them believe that women are weaker than male counterparts in intellectual abilities. I regretfully say that even within the Christian community, there is doubt about their spiritual abilities as well. In general, Arab society (including the Christian community) does not believe that women are as productive as men in the secular marketplace or in ministry and that they are incapable of making wise decisions."

Second Factor: The Arab culture reduces the value of women to her physical person alone
"This painful view of the woman distorts her relationship with her body. As she views herself as society does, she then has either to go to the

extreme and feel that her body is everything she owns so she uses it for gain, or she is ashamed that her body brings disgrace upon her so she tries to hide it, hates it, ignores it, and rejects the fact that she needs it.

In fact, this view of the woman starts at the moment that we think of her as sexually attractive and that she needs to hide her body. "Honor of the family" usually results in locking the woman up and hiding her away from society. That is because they believe there are those who will succeed in seducing and leading her astray, thereby causing disaster for her family."

Third Factor: The constant feeling that she is a burden

Dr. Samuel describes the young lady's belief that she is a burden to her family. "The minute a girl arrives into a family, she feels that she is trouble for that family, and that she is not a beautiful addition to it who is beloved and welcomed but rather a burden who may one day bring them shame or dishonor.

Therefore, we find that the family has this constant desire to marry off their daughters and direct them to give marriage the utmost priority in their lives. Marriage for a woman becomes more important than her work or education and the male alone inherits these advantages."

This way of thinking hinders the woman's ability to achieve many things. Men alone have the right to education, employment, and decision-making. How can that be fair? If the Arab woman thinks back to her childhood, what would she remember? Would she find that her warmth, self-esteem, and contribution to this world really matter? Can these painful memories help her to build a better future?"

To answer these questions, I want to quote this segment from the novel, "Banat Isma'il". Observe these thoughts and memories of an Arab women:

"And as it is the custom of all families who have girls, those time-bombs, as they say, you will fear for them a fear that is like no other; fear of the neighbors, friendships, television, windows and books. And from the fear of those moments of being alone where you can get busted. As if it were a crime to sit alone with yourself for a short period of time to reflect on what they did to you and what they carved in you of traits and customs, values and traditions. They left those in you in the same way they place things on shelves with no order. Hands which do not recognize the beauty; they do not make it and do not keep it. As a result, you become a stranger to yourself and do not recognize who you are because you did not participate even once, in making yourself the person you are.

Governments and families protect us from mixing together; mixing of the two sexes, mixing of cultures, mixing of nations and mixing of knowledge. This is because mixing with those will make you compare, discover, know and then you will rebel and revolutionize, and this is what they do not want you to do."

REACTIONS OF WOMEN TO OPPRESSION
Zaynab is the worst mistress of all. Here is her story:

Zaynab lived in Upper Egypt and was married to a man who humiliated her for years. He would bring women to their home for sex and would always ask Zaynab to take the children to the next room and lock the door.

Zaynab would cry when she heard their laughter and moaning. Her husband was buried so deeply in his sinful life that he showed no remorse, ignored the values of his faith and rejected Zaynab's requests for divorce. She finally submitted to her destiny with this man when he obtained custody of their children.

Her suffering lasted for years until her husband suffered a brain aneurism at the age of 45. He became completely paralyzed and dependent on Zaynab to feed, clothe and nurse him. She considered his affliction as vengeance from God and justice towards her. It was then that she began her journey of revenge. She would send her children outside to play with neighbors in order to invite men to her home to dance naked and have sexual relations with them in front of her disabled husband. Then she would whisper these words to him: "This is a taste of what you did to me for years."

Zaynab's reputation was well known among the men in town and they would say, "If you want pleasure, go to Zaynab's house." Despite her behavior, no men reported her to the Behavior Police since her brother had a very significant position in that department.

One day, Zaynab's daughter fell ill and begged her mother to let her stay home and sleep. Zaynab locked the door but when the dancing began, her sleepless daughter was devastated to see her mother's revengeful acts against the father through the keyhole.

Zaynab had been so humiliated when her husband had shouted to her, "Are you even a woman?" while he had sex with other women that she now turned the tables on him and said,

"Now you know who the woman of all women is and that men follow me to seek pleasure!" She would even ask him to take the children to the neighbor's house, knowing that he was unable to do so.

This story exposes the ugliness created by a man who demeaned his wife and through her retaliation, leaves damaged children who have already suffered under oppression.

Although Zaynab's actions are shockingly unexpected, other women may react differently according to each situation. An act of rebellion by women like this may come at the cost of her life.

The most common reaction to oppression is for a woman to tame her mind to accept her reality. Dr. Samuel states, "Taming the mind here causes a negative response, not a positive one. The natural reaction for the mind is to be able to say no to oppression and reject it entirely. The difficulty arises when the mind is tamed and the mentality of abuse is accepted. The mind then becomes convinced that the reality is unchangeable. As a result, the person gives in to oppression and adapts to it, and this is the tragedy."

We can compare this to the training of the mind of a lion that is unaccustomed to defeat. When a lion is first tamed, he will show his teeth and nails until the tamer effectively trains the animal to comply with his wishes. Thus the animal is forcefully conditioned to submit and obey with the use of cruel tactics.

The programming of the human mind in this way creates a toxic victim-mentality, as the oppressed person views his circumstances as normal and something to which he must become accustomed. Dr. Samuel further states: "A woman might succeed in taming her mind and convince herself that the situation cannot be improved upon, but the natural emotion that God created inside her keeps crying out from within."

The best example of human "taming" is when a woman is obliged to wear a hijab when she leaves the house. She justifies this action by convincing herself that "the pearl should stay hidden inside the oyster and must not show itself." Through this programming, a woman gives in to this accepted reality rather than taking decisive action to change her circumstances or rebel against this injustice. We see a stronger resistance against oppression in Arab children rather than in older people because it is harder for children to tame their minds. As children become older they lose their resistance to oppression as the influence of society intensifies.

If a woman loses hope in her ability to change her circumstances, she falls into despair and helplessness results since she sees no solution to her conflict. Dr. Samuel finds, "Women in the Arab world frequently seek the help of physicians for treatment, but in most cases there is no physical cause found for their ailment. I find that the cause of affliction in these cases is the failure to be treated for the oppression they suffer."

The woman also demonstrates her opposition to female abuse. Dr. Samuel clarifies in his research, "What we find is that she keeps yelling "I am subjugated, I am oppressed" in the faces of men and society. Certainly this will not solve the problem, but at least the problem's presence is acknowledged."

Another reaction to oppression is self-pity. Sadness is a natural way women respond to oppression. I notice this state of mind in most of the women whom I counsel. Feelings of sorrow become a woman's dominant way of thinking in these circumstances.

Dr. Samuel states: "At the beginning, self-pity starts as a feeling, but as time passes and because she does not find anyone to listen to her or sympathize with her, she stays in this state of permanent sadness and is prevented from moving forward."

Even if the oppression ends and the woman moves to a better environment and ultimately finds someone to love her, her sorrow will never diminish.

Self-pity may take a physical form such as a bent spine from not sitting erectly. This curvature of the spine may call for long-term physical therapy and exercise to restore good posture. As self-pity becomes chronic, the woman may need psychological treatment and even intensive care.

DO WOMEN EVEN REALIZE THAT THEY ARE EXPERIENCING OPPRESSION?

Now that we have discussed the causes of the oppression of women and the physical and mental effects it has, do we know whether the Arab woman even realizes that she is experiencing mental persecution? Does she know that she has an altered range of emotions as her permanent state of mind?

Dr. Samuel sums this up in the statement below:
"Sadly enough, a lot of women think that this is the normal way to live. When Abraham Lincoln issued his proclamation freeing the slaves in the America, many of them rejected the creed because they had become

accustomed to slavery as the natural course of events. Just like the slaves, many Arab women do not realize that they are living under oppression in spite of the severity of their suffering."

In order to paint a better picture of this mentality, let us go back to Zaynab's story. When her husband began to commit adultery she made no attempt to reach out for help for fear of repercussion towards her or her children. She endured this abusive behavior for years since she considered her social status to be beneath that of her husband. When her husband became paralyzed all Zaynab's repressed emotions surfaced in the form of extreme vengeance.

Dr. Samuel makes this strong point about the manipulation of the mind: "Taming the mind is one of the worst practices in the Arab world. If I am forced to believe in the status quo, then I do not have to live with the agony that the status quo is wrong. Thus, I do not have to challenge oppression and settle for the fact that nothing can be done to change it."

Dr. Samuel wrote this poem to the daughter he wished he had fathered: "My pain follows you when you embrace your school bag to your chest to hide your femininity. You were taught that nobody should see you; that you should be ashamed of your body and your femininity and now you live under oppression. Now when you walk in the street or ride in a car you think that people glance at you and strip you naked with their eyes."

SURRENDER WITHOUT HESITATION

We stated earlier that a woman tames her mind to accept oppression but is there any hope for change?

Perhaps women in Arab culture have given up on finding female leaders who could effectively stand up for their rights. Perhaps this is the fundamental reason we are not seeing any progress in the treatment of women, even though globalization has allowed us to observe other experiences, achievements and successes for women in other cultures.

Globalization has shown us the equal treatment of men and women and the protection of the fundamental rights of women in other societies. The educated elite within our society must be aware of the problems of Arab women and are capable of defending their rights.

Dr. Samuel comments: "I am embarrassed to say that this educated elite who defend women's rights in public do not treat women in their own homes as if they have these rights."

Nevertheless, we should not lose hope in our leaders. We know that even though the oppression of women is going from bad to worse in our society, we hear about influential women and their successes every day. They continue to rebel against oppression and intellectual inequality to achieve lives filled with education and awareness.

BROKEN BODIES AND EMOTIONAL NUMBNESS
We have discussed the impact of psychological oppression on a woman and now let's delve deeper to see the impact on both her physical body and emotions.

1. Effect on Emotions:
Dr. Samuel states: "When real oppression begins the emotional reaction is denial, so a woman suppresses her sadness. Since her emotional needs such as dignity, acceptance and freedom are unsatisfied, she suffers from emotional freezing or numbness."

We can see that a woman might easily fall prey to a person who waves at her on the road or performs any other trick that might satisfy her need for acceptance. This delusional mindset leads to one of the most relevant causes of emotional heartbreak among Arab females. Seeking fulfillment outside of marriage is not only limited to single women and can result in shocking emotional abuse by the perpetrator.

A woman does not verbalize her feelings because society is not interested in listening. Thus her anger is suppressed and infects her children, causing mental instability in the family and in future generations.

2. Impact on her Body:
The body as well as the mind is in bad shape. Dr. Samuel states: "Oppression does not manifest itself as a physical disease, but it creates a feeling of despair and lack of hope, depriving one of freedom and killing ambition. Negative emotions will not harm the body unless they remain constantly suppressed. The expression of emotion is healthy. Negative emotions eventually transform into passive energy that will find a way to damage the body."

HEALTHY REACTIONS
We must first discuss healthy responses to oppression that women must adopt. Dr. Samuel suggests that women must reject lies spread about them in society and take care of their physical bodies by loving their femininity

and entire body. They must also demonstrate that they are just as important as any man and are not defined by their bodies alone.

Dr. Samuel further states: "When women excel in matters of politics, culture, science or literature they improve society and participate in its advancement. When they achieve what men have not accomplished then the culture will take notice. They must believe that they not only have a body, but that they have a brain, intellect and a will and may even surpass men in both their abilities and accomplishments."

Practical Solutions:
The absence of hope keeps women in an oppressive state because they know their longing for change is out of reach. When civil institutions step up to the plate, women can emerge as pioneers. This could be revolutionary! We could see distinguished women who have freed themselves from the grip of oppression be elevated to the status of exceptional role models in Arab culture. Their positive contributions will prove to be indispensable and pave the way for other women to follow. The gate of hope will open wide for every young woman to confront abuse at the beginning of her life journey. Dr. Samuel provides these practical solutions:

1. Going Back to the Past
The solution to any problem begins with the analysis of the root of the problem. Dr. Samuel proposes training the mind: "The solution begins by connecting with the child inside us. Each person has experienced circumstances since childhood that create subconscious reactions to stress, deprivation and difficult situations that have been suppressed. Even though these situations have long ceased to exist, they should have been addressed in the childhood years."

Dr. Samuel puts forth the example of a woman who suffers from extreme shyness and the feeling of humiliating inferiority in the eyes of her culture. This woman must think of the child inside her and recall her life journey back to when she first became shy because of her femininity and the need to hide her body. Then she should try to remember what she wished her parents would have said to her.

Perhaps she would have wished her father would have said: "I am proud of you because you are my daughter and I want you to cherish and protect your body because it is a gift from God and there is nothing unclean or shameful about it."

Perhaps the woman could have heard positive affirmation from any role model that would have caused her to think anything other than that "It is shameful for people to see your body."

Perhaps she would have heard, "If you are seriously looking for a solution to emotional abuse, you must believe that you are one of the best creations God has made. Be proud of yourself and reject negative feelings. This belief will impact your future decision-making process."

2. Expressing Feelings
Our society can refuse to let us verbalize our emotions but it cannot deprive us from writing about our feelings on paper. Dr. Samuel states, "When a woman is overwhelmed by feelings of oppression she should express them verbally to somebody whom she trusts. If that is not possible, she should write about them in a notebook every day and not ignore her feelings. Writing can help release her negative thoughts and help her remember the things that made her cry. A woman has the right to cry and it is also a healthy outlet for release."

3. Knowledge is the Foundation of Every Development
Knowledge brings change and solidifies the importance of a woman's self-awareness. She must learn from her body and acknowledge fluctuating hormones from childhood and adolescence to maturity and menopause.

Dr. Samuel states, "Increasing a woman's educational awareness increases her ability to protect herself and maintain her physical health through exercise and increase the likelihood of safeguarding her psychological health. A woman's attention to her diet and daily activities enables her to accept her body in a positive way."

When a woman reaches a level of positive self-awareness, she will become more capable of rejecting harmful thoughts. She will feel more confident in demanding freedom and equality while defending her rights, taking responsibility for mistakes and refusing to be shamed by her culture. I firmly believe that this strong woman can exist. We can all work toward elevating women to a higher status and see strength in numbers. Just as the Domino Effect works, unjust ideas can topple one another.

4. Support Groups

Despite this bleak look at the oppression of women, we cannot deny that Arab society has become somewhat enlightened and is recognizing the importance of listening to what woman have to say on this matter.

Dr. Samuel suggests that the church should encourage support groups, especially those related to women. The church also must acknowledge that women are under assault in our Arab world and that they need support networks to help heal from the abuse of both intentional and non-intentional aggression. These networks provide a significant psychological benefit by bringing like-minded people together to share their pain and suffering. Dr. Samuel adds:

"When support groups adopt scientific methods for healing they do not depend on preaching or educational programs and thus provide safe environments where every person may freely express his or her emotions. I used this approach in Cairo and Alexandria and the results were overwhelming. When a woman feels safe she can express her emotions and improve her psychological health tremendously. Many of the situations of these women have improved in unusual ways through participation in support groups."

Members of our society need to realize that when a woman lives under oppression this leads to the birth of oppressed nations. In other words, when a wife feels threatened, the relationship with her husband becomes impaired and the children in turn will be damaged because of the dysfunctional blueprint established by the culture.

What benefit do we reap when women sustain constant abuse? Do the members of our society not realize the harm that spreads, polluting our river at the source? There is no better solution than for us to wake up from our cultural stupor and begin to respect and value women. Our Arab culture must leave old customs behind and recognize the huge impact that women have on our society in order to heal our wounds and transform our society for the betterment of all.

Dr. Samuel professes: "The church will not revive unless the woman takes back her actual role. She is the source of society and society is the source of our church. If she lives under oppression so does our society, which will remain so unless the woman is liberated. There is tremendous promise for the church in freedom for women as they play a most crucial role."

Despite many adversities, we have the hope that more strong young women will emerge to contribute their efforts to elevate the status of women in our society. Perhaps they will inspire millions of young ladies to attain their dreams as well. This movement depends on women who become empowered to be pioneers in their field of expertise and pave the way for others to follow. They will provide excellent role models showing sound judgment and ascribe to the duties of people of religious faith.

References

http://www.tathwir.com/2013/12/psyco-complex.html

Ruba Rihani

THE WOMAN IN CHRISTIANITY

TALES FROM CHRISTIAN REALITY

There is widespread discrimination against women in our culture and women pay a great price for their femininity. Women take responsibility for all aspects of daily life in the home. If women are widowed there is nobody to provide for her children and if she wants to remarry she faces another form of shaming. If she is single, married, or widowed, the honor of the family is the medal that she wears on her chest and to ensure that badge does not get ripped off she must submit to the rigid requirements of her culture's tradition and customs.

I long witnessed men abuse women and realize that this act is not limited to a specific country or region, but it is a global issue. This abuse and discrimination against Christian women has gone on long enough. You may agree that the Christian woman suffers financially, politically and socially, but do you know exactly what happens in Christian households and what exactly is her role in the church?

In an attempt to familiarize myself with the needs of the Christian woman both in her home and social environment I questioned a group of young women in a church setting and these are the responses that I received:

1. "As a child, I was denied schooling. I grew up sadly watching my young brothers attend school and college. I would stand in front of the mirror and blame myself for my lack of education and thus I resorted to becoming a servant in my own home."
2. "My parents removed me from school to marry at age fourteen. I begged both my father and mother not to do this, but I was

ignored. When I married I was thrust into the domain of my husband's family who controlled my decisions and his income and I am still in this situation today."

3. "This is not fair. Why does my family show favoritism toward my brother over me? Why is he not held accountable for his mistakes like I am? Why don't they give me the same space and freedom that they give him? He leaves home whenever he wishes and returns late at night. Why can't my parents treat me the same way? I would be satisfied with only half the amount of freedom that he has."

In regard to their opinions concerning honor killings only one of twenty women said that she objected to all kinds of honor crimes and the rest agreed that any woman who dishonors her family should be killed.

In this last chapter of my book, I will address the main reason leading to the current issue of women's suffering and explore the stance of the Christian church concerning women. Then I will explain God's plan for women and offer a solution that can make the church more effective in bringing about change to conform with the view of women as outlined in scripture. I will also discuss how a woman has a mission from God to pursue both spiritual and social change to set an example for others to follow.

WHAT EXACTLY IS THE PROBLEM?

The suffering of women in the church and society began thousands of years ago after the fall of Adam and Eve in the Garden of Eden. The Ancient Egyptian Civilization was the pioneering culture of the humanistic treatment of women. The Egyptian woman during the rule of the Pharaohs had the right of inheritance and took charge of her family during the absence of her husband. Women were regarded as less flawed than men and their husbands put the ownership of all their possessions in the name of their wives. Children carried their mother's surname and women were always superior to men. Husbands pledged obedience to wives in all matters outlined in the marriage contract.

There was no place for female dominance in other cultures and the position of women began to weaken gradually in other civilizations such as the Babylonian, Assyrian, Greek and Roman. They considered women to be unclean, mortal, animal, or having no spirit. The woman was only to serve and never allowed to laugh or speak or she would be silenced like a camel or a dog since she was considered to be a product of the devil. Socrates once said that: "The existence of the woman is the largest source of crisis and the collapse in the world. The woman is like a poisonous tree; it appears to be attractive, but birds will immediately die once they eat of it's fruit."

Even the Jewish culture was not exempt from a negative view of women. Enslaved Jewish women were restricted from providing testimony as a witness. Under Jewish inheritance law, women were not allowed to inherit their father's property unless he had no son. The wife was also prevented from receiving her husband's inheritance which was passed to the closest male relative in the husband's clan (Numbers 27:1-11). Men could divorce their wives for any silly reason but women were only allowed to request a divorce in unusual cases. (Deuteronomy 24:1-3).

From birth, Jewish males were favored over females and women lacked religious rights and honor. Jewish men began their day with prayer while women and slaves were exempt and men would even pray: "Lord, you are blessed for not creating me among the Gentiles or as a woman."

This degradation of the female continued in all civilizations throughout history. As for Arab society, without a doubt, patriarchy is dominant. Regretfully, we see this erroneous masculine attitude deeply engraved even in the heart and the mind of the Christian man that overlooks the highly esteemed view of women as shown in God's Word. (I will discuss this later in the chapter.) We see the Christian man marginalize both the role and position of women while claiming to be protecting their honor. In Arab society, the Christian man views the woman as lacking and practices dominance toward her in all aspects of life.

I remember well the day my sisters and I with our only brother went to the Orthodox Court to process our inheritance upon the death of my father. As we were filing the paperwork the clerk said: "As you know, the male inherits double the amount the female does." My sisters and I nodded our heads in agreement. I also recall what happened after my grandfather passed. His wealth was estimated to be in the millions, and my mother, the only female among three siblings, did not inherit anything. She didn't even receive what the existing law allowed; half of her brothers' inheritance. My mother isn't the only Christian woman who did not receive her rightful inheritance and her daughters are not the only females in our community who had the misfortune of receiving only half the inheritance the male siblings received.

Unfortunately, this injustice extends to our Christian courts regardless of which denominational rules apply since courts follow the Islamic Law rulings even though they are not obligated to do so. The men in charge of these courts carry on with old customs and traditions and support legislation that fulfills their interests and desires to keep inheritance and family possessions in the hands of male descendants.

Many poor Christian women live in denial of their identities and even conceal family names so their religion cannot be known. These acts of repression recently occurred in Iraq, Syria, Egypt's countryside, and some of the areas in Jordan where unemployment and discrimination against women have increased. The Middle Eastern Woman is still a second-class citizen whether she's a Christian or not. Conflicting interpretations of Paul's writings concerning women and their role in teaching within the church create even more obstacles.

THE STRUGGLE BETWEEN CULTURE AND FAITH

The current state of the Christian community is not healthy since it is a community that is not living according to God's will. Psalm 22:23 tells us to fear and glorify the Lord and Psalm 84:11 tells us the Lord bestows favor and honor on those who walk blamelessly. Our churches are not living up to these standards.

The young church women who were in support of honor crimes were surprised when I told them that Jesus forgave the sinful woman who anointed his feet with perfume (Luke 8:48) and that scripture does not support honor killings in the New Testament. These women had not only judged the behaviors of afflicted women but also believed it was necessary for the death penalty to cleanse their shame, when we know for certain that Christ atoned for the sins of believers at the cross. (Jn 3:16).

Why does the woman who gets caught committing adultery get killed, but the man faces no backlash when he commits the same act? Is it more important to preserve the family's honor or to glorify God in our families? There is a tremendous imbalance between our culture and religious faith. It seems that culture trumps belief!

Many Christian assemblies completely prohibit combining the sexes during worship as is the custom in the Middle East. This separation makes women feel as if they are isolated from the rest of the world. Even though some churches allow couples to sit next to each other during the services, most do not. In many villages and small towns women do not even attend funerals, memorial services or wakes.

GOD'S PLAN FOR THE WOMAN

1. In the beginning

To understand the nature of the relationship God desired between the woman and the man, let's go back to the beginning and the book of

Genesis. We find that female inferiority was not part of God's design when he created the man:

"So, God created man in his own image; in the image of God He created him; male and female He created them. God blessed them and said to them, 'Be fruitful and increase in number; fill the earth and subdue it. Rule over the fish of the sea and the birds of the air and over every living creature that moves on the ground.'" Genesis 1:27-28 (NIV)

In these verses, both man and woman stand equally in front of God without discrimination; they are both together in life and work. They are together in nature and authority representing God on earth. God's criteria did not change after the fall, nor did his view towards Adam and Eve.

In the Old Testament, the Lord allowed women to conduct worship and services in a way that even the closest men to Him could not practice. In comes Miriam, a prophetess, Moses' sister, and the leader of the Lord's people. Miriam was the worship and praise leader, and she praised the Lord with timbrel and danced in front of him with her song. (Exodus 15:20- 21). She prophesied during formal meetings for the Lord's people in the presence of men who listened through her mouth to the Lord's word in the Holy Spirit. They had to obey according to what she said because God himself inspired her. "Then Miriam the prophetess, Aaron's sister, took a tambourine in her hand, and all the women followed her, with tambourines and dancing. Miriam sang to them: 'Sing to the Lord, for He is highly exalted. The horse and its rider He has hurled into the sea.'" (Ex 15:20-21)

The Book of Judges tells us about Deborah, one of the Judges of the Israelites appointed by the Lord to return his people to Him and stand against His enemies. A judge and prophet for God's people had to be well-versed in the Law to teach and give counsel to others concerning daily life problems and must also issue rulings and verdicts.

Ruth, Rahab, and Esther were biological ancestors of Christ. Esther, who became the queen of Persia and Media, used her influence to save her people from their enemy, Haman.

In the book of Numbers (27:1-11), we read the story of the daughters of Zelophehad who stood in front of Moses and the Israelites asking for the rights to their father's inheritance. The Book of 1 Samuel describes the wisdom of Abigail and the book of 2 Kings tells us about the prophetess Huldah. Huldah was asked by the king's priest what the Lord's word was concerning the king and his people. These verses, in addition to many others, confirm that women had a direct relationship to the Kingdom of God. They are given the name "evangelists." Scripture states: "I will pour out my Spirit on all people. Your sons and daughters will prophesy." (Acts 2:17-18)

2. Since the coming of the Christ

At the time when Christ lived on earth, the Greeks, Romans, and Jews all believed that women were of lower status. It's no surprise that the divorce phenomenon was prevailing. In the Greek era, the woman was considered immoral. During the Roman period, she suffered at the hands of man's brutality. In the society where Jesus lived, the man was superior while the woman was of lower rank than her husband. She had no education or religious teaching at all.

In contrast to this background, Jesus Christ respected the woman and gave her value. He liberated her from the burden of inferiority and enslavement during his time on earth. The woman had part of Christ's teachings reserved only for her. We clearly see his position toward women in his teachings about divorce and lust in "The Sermon on the Mount" in the Gospel of Mark (Mark 10). His teachings about this matter were strange words for their ears and contrary to their customs. He made marriage a Holy Covenant between the husband and the wife comparing it to the covenant between Christ and the church. Jesus also stressed the importance of unity in marriage and his disapproval of adultery, lust and immorality.

Christ appreciated the incredible gifts that God had bestowed upon women and treated them all with respect and kindness. One example is the healing of Peter's mother-in-law from fever (Matthew 8:14) and the healing of the bleeding woman who touched the hem of his cloak. (Matthew 9:20-21) Jesus told her, "Take heart daughter, your faith has healed you."

There is also the story of the woman who was bent over and could not straighten up for eighteen years (Luke 13:11) due to an evil spirit. He called her forward and put his hands on her and she immediately straightened up.

Christ's compassion toward women is also shown when he sympathized with the widow of Nain in her sadness and pain, and raised her son from the dead Luke 7:12). When Jesus was on the cross, he showed his compassion toward his mother when he commanded John, the beloved apostle to care for his mother on earth after his return to heaven: "This is your mother." (John 19:25-27) are the words he spoke to John.

Jesus applauded the faith of Canaanite women. One begged him, "Lord, Son of David, have mercy on me! My daughter is suffering terribly from demon-possession." Jesus' disciples asked him to send her away. After declaring that he was sent only to the lost sheep of Israel, she continued to plead and he answered her, "Woman, you have great faith! Your request is granted." And from that moment the woman's daughter was healed. (Matthew 15:21-28 NIV).

Jesus sat by the treasury and watched people put their offerings into the temple treasury. In the Gospel of Mark, many wealthy people threw in large amounts of money, but a poor widow came forth and contributed two small copper coins, worth only a few cents. Jesus applauded her in front of his disciples and said to them: "I tell you the truth, this poor widow has put more into the treasury than all the others. They all gave out of their wealth; but she, out of her poverty, put in everything – all she had to live on."

We see his encouragement to Mary who chose a better role than Martha and sat by his feet to learn from his teachings, a practice that contradicted all prevailing customs concerning women. In the story of the woman who lived a sinful life, Jesus allowed her to kiss his feet and wipe them with her hair and wet them with her tears (Luke 7:36-50).

Jesus also elevated women when he compared the Kingdom of God to the yeast a women hid in three containers of flour until it worked all through the dough.

The Lord's search for the sinner is portrayed in the lost coin parable (Luke 15:8-10). The woman searched carefully until she found the piece. Similarly, on the topic of praying without ceasing, Jesus discussed the mother's persistence with the unjust judge until she was granted her request. The Lord also compared the joy of the resurrection to the pain of a pregnant woman in labor and her delight with the baby upon his birth.

Jesus showed his divine design for women and restored honor and dignity to them when he allowed them to join his missionary journey. In the Gospel of Luke, we find a list of women who went out with Jesus and supported his ministry with their money. Women stood by him at the cross and witnessed his burial when other male disciples ran away. The Lord Jesus led the campaign for changing customs to fulfill God's plan for the woman. He came to set the captive free and spread justice among the people.

Women accompanied Jesus from his birth in Bethlehem to his crucifixion on the Mount of Golgotha. The presence of the women in

Jesus' life was unusual and felt abnormal to the Jews and their customs in the Old Testament (John 8:2-12). Even Jesus' disciples were surprised when they saw Jesus speaking to a Samaritan woman. We cannot help but mention Mary Magdalene from whom Jesus cast out seven demons, thus curing her. (Luke 8:2).

3. In the letters of the New Testament

The main verse which addresses equality in the Apostle Paul's letters is Galatians 3:28. "There is neither Jew nor Greek, slave nor free, male nor female, for you are all one in Christ Jesus."

If we are all created in his image, then there is no difference between one and the other. Paul here refers to the words of the Jews. In his Bible commentary on The New Testament, Father Antounius Fikry also makes the point, "Paul here quotes from the Morning Prayer Book for them when they pray. They pray thanking God that he did not create them Gentiles, slaves or women; these are considered the source of impurity."

Concerning the woman's role in marriage, here is a reading from Paul the Apostle in his letter to the Ephesians (which is considered to be one of the most significant teachings on the relationship between husbands and wives):

"Submit to one another out of reverence for Christ. Wives, submit to your own husbands as to the Lord. For the husband is the head of the wife as Christ is the head of the church, his body, of which he is the Savior. Now as the church submits to Christ, so also wives should submit to their husbands in everything. Husbands, love your wives, just as Christ loved the Church and gave himself up for her to make her holy, cleansing her by the washing with water through the Word, and to present her to himself as a radiant Church, without stain or wrinkle or any other blemish, but holy and blameless. In this same way, husbands ought to love their wives as their own bodies. He who loves his wife loves himself," (Ephesians 5:21-28).

Due to the problems with marital relationships in those days, we find some of the most essential instructions Paul the Apostle gave in his letter to the Ephesians; the women were forced to obey, but Paul encouraged them to submit to their husbands as the Church submitted to Christ. He requested the same act from the husband, as the submission of the man to the woman includes a sacrificing love as Christ's love toward his bride, the Church. This gesture translates into mutual submission built on love and respect.

The New Testament points to the loyalty of its followers, one to the other, in the context of mutually accepting each other, sharing thoughts and the exchange of opinions, instead of blind and absolute obedience. Here, Paul the Apostle saw the importance of submission within the family, where the wife must submit to her husband. The children will observe this submission and learn to submit to their father and mother, and the family becomes in its unity, a role model as to what the Church is to become; united in love. The husband must love his wife as he loves his body, thus removing the wife from a place of inferiority. The man who feels Christ's love for him must love his wife with the same compassion. Christ loved the Church while she was still in sin, and so the man must love his wife not because she has all the right qualities, but because she is his wife, a gift given to him by the Lord.

As we have learned, the Lord teaches us that in Christ Jesus there is no difference between a man and a woman, a slave or free person, between the races, or young and old. When the Lord provides his gifts, he does not look to the gender of the person, but he looks to the heart first and sees how eager the person is to serve, exalt, and glorify his name in complete obedience, regardless of whether the person is a man or a woman.

INFLUENCE IN MINISTRY
If we look into a woman's day and see the roles she plays in all aspects of her life, the church, the family, and society, we see that her work is unending. The woman does all the household chores, bears and cares for children, feeds them, and directs them concerning proper hygiene and manners.

In the morning, the woman prepares breakfast, gets the children ready for school and then heads to work. In the evening she returns home, gets dinner ready, washes the dishes, takes care of the children and their homework and then tucks the children into bed. On the weekend, she does the laundry, cleans the house and shops for the household. These tasks are all done in addition to her social duties, whether they involve cooking at home or for the sick or entertaining guests. The total sum of her daily tasks is equal to about sixteen hours. But the woman's contribution doesn't stop with her family; I firmly believe she is the one who takes care of our entire society. This is quite a noble role for her to fill, and as we have seen, she has come a long way. In the beginning, God created her first to become Adam's helper, and later her duty evolved into caring for the family when they were granted children. Although the woman plays a central role as caretaker, this is not the only mission God has given to her.

The woman, whether a mother or educator, despite her social status or her career, plays the most significant role in the reform and the development of society. Therefore, the man must support the woman. Likewise, the woman has the duty to help other women in or outside of the church's walls.

Paul's letters are filled with references about women who served the Lord. Let's look at Lydia. She was a woman who loved the Lord and hosted the apostles in her home. Then there was Priscilla, whom Paul the Apostle called, "My fellow worker in Christ Jesus in God's ministry." Priscilla and her husband hosted a church in their home for believers and performed numerous tasks in their service of these people.

We see then the Gospel of Jesus Christ views the woman, in complete equality with the man, whether as mother, daughter or wife. The value of the woman is also a reflection of her relationship with her father, husband, and son.

In Christianity, the woman is to the man as the church is to Christ. The natural difference between the man and woman are biological and they are to complete each other in body, mind, and heart. The Christian woman is tasked from birth, as the man, with performing religious rituals just as Jesus did, surrounded by male and female disciples during his ministry and journeys.

The Bible probably has not complimented any other individual in the way Jesus exalted the woman who poured the expensive perfume on his head. (Mark 14:9): "I tell you the truth, wherever the Gospel is preached throughout the world, what she has done will also be told, in memory of her."

Why did he compliment her? He did that because the men of that time were unable to comprehend the honor that this woman had bestowed upon Jesus, and rebuked the woman at her extravagance. The Lord was aware of the woman's gratuitous gesture and welcomed it. He proclaims that in her love toward Him led by the spirit, she performed a prophetic act that no one else shared. She gave away all that she possessed in preparation for his burial even before his crucifixion and death had occurred.

What excites me about the woman in general, is that no matter what her background or culture, she will not surrender to her situation. She remains resilient in her spirit and soul. She stands firm like a lonely tree in the desert, and despite the harsh environment, scarcity of water, and lack of nutrition from the earth, it is always green and alive. This tree shadows whomever seeks rest. The tree even sometimes penetrates the rocks to keep its branches above ground. The woman has resilience, a strong will, and the power to change. She struggles to survive while defending herself and her children. I have met with many women over the years who suffered numerous adversities in their lives; and even more so now due to the current political and economic conflicts in the Arab world. These women, however, have not allowed hardship to stop them. They have shown the will and persistence to move on whether their struggles involve disease, divorce, displacement or poverty.

THE DISPARITY BETWEEN REALITY AND HOPE
I listened for hours to Lina's story. She had this to say about her pastor:

"He did not have the experience or the knowledge to help me and my husband solve our problems. I was forced to go to another denomination to proceed with the divorce. My pastor's main concern was to not damage the reputation of our church. He wanted me to keep the matter confidential so the congregation would not learn of our story. He even said that he only knows how to preach from the pulpit and does not know how to deal with interpersonal problems, especially regarding marriage."

When Lina's marriage ended, the church took the stand that she was rebellious and she had not treated her husband fairly.

What makes Lina's situation different from that of any other Christian woman or even those who deal with disparity when it comes to inheritance? What makes the Christian family an example to follow in a male-dominant culture?

It seems that the church is out of touch with reality and our daily life issues. The church does not teach about the power of Divine Truth that changes our wrongful mindset regarding the treatment of women from birth to death. We must highlight the role of the church in guiding the modern family to assign just and equal roles to marriage partners. Family unification can only occur if the church addresses fair treatment of both parties. Both men and women need counseling in regard to marital disputes, domestic violence and intimate relations. From my own observation of the current state of these matters, women's needs are being neglected both publicly and privately.

I see that Christian leaders fail to provide counseling and Christian guidance before or after marriage due to lack of experience and preparation for this role. As a result marital problems escalate. Ideally ministry could possibly redirect their marital cases to professionals or counseling centers (if they even exist). Who is the first to suffer? No doubt the women absorbs the burden since she faces the church's pressure to not divorce. The church believes it is best for her to accept her situation.

Looking at the Christian faith, Christ is the foundation and the central pillar in the work of Divine Grace, and the grace principle and the shame principle are at odds with each other. Christian pastors do not encourage the implementation of the Divine Grace principle. Thus, we find the Christian family in the Middle East is in a struggle with the chaos created by a culture overcome with shame and guilt, which affects other religions. There is absolutely no guidance, education or care regarding this matter by any Christian authority in the Middle East.

We share our conflicts at the Arab Woman Today Center. We hold workshops, forums, symposiums, and conferences for Christian women so we can address the cultural and social struggles and the mechanisms that can improve them. These support networks have helped spread awareness among women, encouraging them to take a decisive stance; first methodically, then practically. The change starts in their households, then moves outwardly to the community.

The most important topics discussed at the center are domestic violence, inheritance, decision making, and communication concerning emotions. Other issues addressed are the healthy expression of personality and the correct interpretation of Christian attitudes as presented in the Bible. Even more significant is the follow-through we do with these women. Individual follow-up for each of these women helps resolve many disputes. We have even had to enlist the cooperation of The Family Protection Association, but our methods are working. The tepid woman who refused to stay silent for fear of her reputation and her children's protection, has been transformed into a confident woman who is able to communicate her needs and put an end to violence.

There are several initiatives that churches can implement to support women in a positive way and help produce emotionally healthy Christian families. Monthly meetings for couples to address family conflicts and methods of raising children can bring open discussions. This support will provide opportunity for couples to learn new and constructive methods to confront any crises that occur between them.

Good citizenship isn't only about paying taxes, protecting national resources, and loving King and country. Good citizenship is manifested in the love of God first, and in loving our neighbors as ourselves. Who is our closest neighbor and relative? Is the woman a near or distant neighbor? What I mean here is not to just state that we love others, but showing our love for others which starts with respecting the woman and ends in sacrificing for her and her children.

The woman cannot understand her value and importance and live with dignity and honor if she cannot accept and respect herself first. Self-respect motivates the woman and gives her the dignity to make changes in her society and helps elevate the church. The man cannot view the woman as equal to him unless there is an outstanding church teaching that offers more balanced gender messages than the out-dated directives men were raised with. Certainly this shift toward equality would alter the way the man sees the woman at home, at work, and in the street.

The church is the place to prepare women for the struggles she will face in life. The church takes care of the children at an early age and morally educates women from the time they are in school until she finishes her academic studies at a college or university. The church prepares her for marriage and embraces her regardless of her social status or background. The church welcomes her to worship and may offer her a leadership position according to her abilities and the needs of the local church body. The church widens the field for her to minister to the congregation.

I sometimes see the unjust customs and traditions of our society become the guiding force for our Christian walk. Secular culture bombards us every day, weakening the influence of the Word of God and even discourages us from receiving the correct teaching and responding properly to it. These customs and habits trail into our churches with us and hinder our understanding of God's word concerning the woman.

Even when women make up only half of the church's congregation, their presence and involvement is 60 - 70 percent. We are amazed by the high participation of women in ministry and spiritual work but question the types of roles offered to these women. We can estimate that a large number of these women will be participating in leadership circles.

The church has a large responsibility to prepare the woman and enable her spiritually, psychologically and even physically. When the church begins to reach out to Arab society, it first sends out the woman, for they know her strength is her ability to communicate and to redeem social relationships for Christ. The church sends her out confident that she is prepared, qualified, respected and honored. The church does not have to search for that quality in the world that does not have Christ's light, as the light of Christ shines through her to the world.

This is what the word of God teaches us about the woman's position, for the Lord's word is true, "Give her the reward she has earned, and let her works bring her praise at the city gate."

References

1. The Woman Throughout the Ages: A. Sahar Abdul Qader al-Labban
2. The Woman Throughout the Ages
3. Fay Smart, "The Woman Who Pleases God"
4. Joanne Crupp, "Woman: God's Plan Not Man's Tradition"
5. Rev. Samuel Zaki, "The Woman in the Bible".
6. B.M. Metzger & M.D. Coogan ،"The Oxford Companion to the Bible" ،Oxford University Press, New York, NY, (1993), P. 806 to 818
7. http://st-takla.org/pub_Bible-Interpretations/Holy-Bible-Tafsir-02-New-Testament/Father Antonious-Fekry/09-Resalet-Ghalatya/Tafseer-Resalat-Ghalatia__01-Chapter-03.html
8. http://www.al-shia.org/html/ara/seyedat/?mod=dinieh&id=134
9. http://www.alukah.net/social/0/27156/

ABOUT THE AUTHOR

Ruba Rihani holds a Bachelor of Journalism and Media from Yarmouk University and a Master of Women's Studies from the University of Jordan. During her studies, she had a dream and a passion for enabling the Arab Woman and motivating her to pursue a better life; instead of a life of humiliation and oppression.
In 1999, she founded Arab Woman today Ministry and continues to run it today.
She began her work with a radio program entitled "The Woman Today" which was broadcast on Trans World Radio. In 2013, she launched the television program "Start from Here" which is currently being broadcast on Sat-7 channel.
Ruba currently lives in Jordan and is married to Rev. Dr. Nabeeh Abbassi, and has three children: Ramzi, Rami and Randy.